PASSION TO PROFITS

Ryan Lee

This book is dedicated to my mother, Beverly Lee,
who passed from cancer in April 2010.

Copyright Notice

Copyright © 2011 by Ryan Lee

ISBN: 978-0-9794187-1-6

Table of Contents

Forward

by Kent Emmons

Are you excited to wake up every morning and look forward to a day filled with fun, adventure, laughs and the freedom to do what you want when you want? The first thing I do every morning is take five minutes before I get out of bed and I think of all of the many things that I am thankful for. My family, my friends, my health and the freedom I have to pretty much do what I want when I want because I have built my business to accommodate MY lifestyle – not someone else's.

I truly feel sorry for people who are stuck working for someone else because, for as much control as they think they have over their lives, they really have very little. They make the amount of money someone else says they can make, They get a raise when someone else says they get a raise and they take vacations when someone else says they can take a vacation. They have absolutely no ownership of their life. And, like I've always said, You are either working to build your own dream or you are working to build someone else's dream. That's why they call it "wage slavery" – because these poor souls are literally slaves. In my opinion being trapped in wage slavery would be a very sad existence. In this day and age, the ability to be financially independent is an absolute must and there has never been a better time to start.

As a TV and radio personality and infomercial host and producer, I am approached daily by people who have "the next great product or service" that they would like me to sell on TV. Some folks have great ideas and others well… not so great. And, sadly, many of the people that are trying to get on TV have those ridiculous get rich quick "programs" that come in the form of a book or DVD series –

and are almost always schemed up by some guy or gal who has never created wealth in any way, let alone, by using their own "new secret way". Around my office we jokingly refer to these scamsters as "gold chain and pinky ring" types. My business was built on 100% credibility so not only have I always turned down requests for meetings with these "money making guru" types, I don't even return their calls.

Then one day last year I got a phone call from my good friend, New York Times best selling author John Assaraf who said, "You need to meet Ryan Lee." Of course, I had heard great things about Ryan for years from other friends of mine but Ryan and I had never met. John told me about Ryan's journey from rags to riches and how he believes that Ryan may be the only credible person in the business opportunity arena with absolute credibility who can actually teach people how they truly can build a business from nothing and grow it quickly into a multi-million dollar enterprise.

Knowing that John is an amazing judge of character, I agreed to meet with Ryan and not only did he turn out to be the real deal in the building a business space – he is far beyond. Yes, he and his wonderful wife Janet built their business from nothing into a multi-million dollar enterprise, but as you'll read in the following pages, they did it with amazing integrity, heart, passion, honesty, and with the absolute purest intentions. He is not one of those blow-hearts you see on TV in the middle of the night sitting on the hood of a rented yellow Ferrari or standing by a swimming pool surrounded by Vegas strippers blabbing about how he "makes up to $50,000 a day on the internet". Ryan is a very conservative, well-grounded family man with 4 amazing young children living the American dream. Ryan Lee IS the real deal. He has created the ultimate blueprint to building a big business on the internet and, unlike most of those idiots you see on late night infomercials, – HE ACTUALLY DID IT by using his own methods.

In this book, Ryan lays out the steps he used when he went from making a few thousand dollars a month to making the millions he makes now. His step-by-step system is so simple and easy that you will be excited and motivated to go out and start your own business and start living the lifestyle you really want. Ryan easily shows you how to tap into what you love doing and how to enjoyably build a business around it. He has done it time and time again for thousands of people. I know this first hand from personally talking to hundreds of his students and by speaking to thousands at his seminars.

In his simple 21-day process you can actually build an empire and literally turn your passion into profits. In this book, Ryan makes taking action easy and fun by showing you how to create your own personal empire. Being a self described "technophobe", Ryan readily admits that he is not a technical whiz, and it is for that reason that he created this system to be so simple that anyone can do it. That's right, you don't need to be a techie!

Ryan is an incredible source of amazing positive energy and I am so delighted that he is making Passion to Profit available to the public and that there is finally a valid, honest, fail proof system available to aspiring entrepreneurs who want to enjoy life while building a multi-million dollar business. I love to see how stoked Ryan and his staff get when they see yet another student go from $11 in their pocket to making their first $20,000 in a very short period of time - and I've witnessed it many times.

I've seen it all and one thing I can tell you for sure – RYAN LEE IS THE REAL DEAL! Seeing success after success with his students and talking to them personally, I am even more excited to tell everyone I know about Passion to Profit.

People often say that there are some things to do and places to go that only people with money get to experience and that those people are a pretty tight knit group of people. I can tell you that is absolutely true. The good news for you is that there is plenty of room for you here in this tight knit group of success. Understand that those of us who built our own wealth were in your shoes not to many years ago. The only thing that truly separates us from you is that we took the first step. And now Ryan Lee, through his program "Passion to Profit" has given you the opportunity to take YOUR first step. We look forward to you joining us!

The Importance of Changing Diapers

I won't hide behind false modesty here: I've had a lot of success, I'm proud of that success, and I'm writing this book to help you achieve the same type of success. I run profitable businesses and I devote more time and energy to my family than most guys in my position.

Currently, I run more than 50 websites. I've built three software companies, a nutritional supplement company, and published dozens of e-books, paid membership sites, DVDs, and other information products. People have traveled all over the world and paid up to $5,000 to attend my workshops, where I teach them how to create their own products and launch their own online businesses.

Many of my students have gone from financial distress to financial success in a matter of months. One, Patrick Beith, had eleven dollars in his checking account when he started using my methods. Within three months, he was earning more than thirty thousand dollars a month. (He makes a lot more than that now.)

Another student of mine, Mike Geary, went from an ordinary personal trainer to earning almost eight figures a year with a popular e-book about fitness.

But here's something few people know about me: I don't possess any skills you don't have. In fact, I'm a pretty ordinary guy. I haven't set my alarm clock in years, and I'm the farthest thing from a workaholic. If I want to see a movie on a weekday afternoon, I see it. Most days I work from my office just a short stroll from my house, but sometimes I do my work from my home office or from my local bookstore. When I do go to my outside office, I get home in time for dinner with my family every night.

I've been married since 2000 to my college sweetheart, Janet, and we have four beautiful children. I've been changing diapers every day since Jordyn was born in 2003. By the time Jacob, born in 2009, is potty-trained, I figure I'll have changed at least one diaper almost every day of my life for eleven consecutive years.

Ryan's 4 children (left to right), Camryn, Jordyn, Lauryn and Jacob

Why am I sharing my diaper diaries with you? Because I want to show that we're more similar than different. We share the same goals and endure the same hassles. If you have the idea that you have to become someone else to achieve financial success I want you to get those thoughts out of your head.

You and I want a rich life, and for me, there's no point in being financially successful if it means sacrificing anything else that's important, starting with my daily involvement in every aspect of family life—right down to the baby's diapers.

Janet Lee's book:
The Daily Doodle

While I'm on the subject of my family, I also want to make it clear that I didn't marry some Stepford wife who has no career or ambitions of her own. Janet earned a Ph.D. in child psychology by the time she was just 25 years old. She's taking a few years away from full-time pursuit of her career to raise our kids, but she's still doing some part time counseling and even wrote her own book, The Daily Doodle.

In other words, we're a two-career couple raising our children together. We wouldn't have it any other way.

A Tale of Two Career Paths

As long as I've told you about my family life, I should tell you about my career. I wasn't born with any superpowers as a businessman, and no one handed me a magical formula for success. In fact, I began my career the usual way—at the bottom.

After I graduated college, I went to work as a recreational therapist and fitness trainer at Blythedale Children's Hospital in Valhalla, New York, where I worked with children of all ages and abilities for more than six years.

That job shifted my outlook on life in a profound way. I saw so many brave young kids facing death who still worked hard in therapy. They didn't want anyone to feel sorry for them. When you know that someone you've worked with and have gotten to like is probably going to die by the end of the day, you realize how trivial most of life's annoyances really are.

What's missing the latest Seinfeld episode or getting stuck in traffic compared to a good life ending at such a young age?

I didn't earn much—I lived in my parents' basement—but the hours were flexible and I had weekends and evenings free. That's when I started my first fitness-training company, which gave me an opportunity to work with healthy clients with a full spectrum of talents and ambitions—regular folks all the way up to elite athletes.

Naturally, as a personal trainer, I needed a website to promote my business. It was 1998, when most people had heard of the Internet but didn't really have firm ideas about what it was or how it could be used for profit. I confess it never occurred to me that I was staking my first claim in the medium that would eventually allow me to become a millionaire. I was just a guy with an active URL, trying to build a personal-training business.

But then a funny thing happened: As I began to add free articles to the site, I saw that people across the country—around the world, even—were finding out about it, enjoying the content, and telling people they knew about it. I was soon bought out by a large Internet company.

Okay, we all know how the Internet works, and we all know stories about small businessmen who became large businessmen when a big company came calling with an open checkbook.

I wasn't one of those businessmen.

I went to work for the company that bought me out. The job lasted all of two months before the company ran out of cash and let everyone go.

Almost all of my compensation was in stock, so when the company went belly-up, the stock was worthless, and I was broke.

The timing couldn't have been worse. I was unemployed for the first time in my life, having left a safe, secure job at the hospital to experience the crazy world of Internet start-ups. And my wedding was just two weeks away.

I hit the pavement and within a week I found a job with another Internet company. I would start as soon as I got back from my honeymoon.

This wasn't just a job to me. I'd be entering the corporate world for the first time. I was no longer a trainer with a website. I was a player in the most exciting and fastest-growing business opportunity of my lifetime.

But just 10 minutes into this new career, I knew I'd made a huge mistake. The first nine minutes at the job were terrific. I couldn't wait to share my ideas on how to build our website with my new boss. When the meeting started, I rattled off one killer idea after another. She, with the skill of a seasoned tennis pro, returned every one of my shots with lethal precision. "No," she said, over and over and over again, until my ideas and enthusiasm were spent.

It was my first morning on the job, but already I could feel the clock ticking away on my corporate ambitions. Seven months later, I got called into the conference room, where my boss and someone from human resources were waiting for me. You know what happened next.

So here's the scorecard: After six years at one job, I was now unemployed for the second time in just nine months.

I was still running a few of my own websites, and they were bringing in some money. I tried my hand in the domain-name game with a site called domainrepo.com. That brought in about $1,000 a month, mostly through advertising and sponsorships. I also did online training through my first site, Complete Conditioning, and that brought in another $500 or so a month. Selling downloadable fitness programs generated an extra $200 a month. So I was doing okay, but wasn't making enough to live on.

This time it took me three months to find a job. The one I landed was at a new alternative high school in the Hunts Point section of the South Bronx. I was given complete freedom to start up a new health and physical education program for the school's poor and at-risk students.

It was (and still is) a very rough neighborhood. Here's an example: I parked my car right in front of the school, and yet my side-view mirrors and turn-signal lights were stolen three different times. Each time it happened, I went to one of the shops in the neighborhood to replace them. (I'm being generous when I call them "shops." They were really just run-down storage sheds.) When I told them what I needed, the proprietors would pull out a big black garbage bag filled with auto parts and sell me back my own lights and mirrors.

Needless to say, the job was challenging. Many of the young teenagers were actively involved in gangs. Most had arrest records. A disturbing number had already become parents. Still, I enjoyed my time there. I connected with a lot of my students, and I was happy when they came to me for advice.

At nights and during my free time, I began to work hard on my websites again. I launched my first paid membership site in late September 2001. (I was going to launch on September 11, but we all know what happened on that horrible day. Our school was right by the water, and we could see the World Trade Center towers burn and then crumble from our windows.)

The website was an instant hit. Revenues increased for nine consecutive months. That's when I took one more leap of faith and left the world of paychecks and employer-provided dental plans to dedicate myself full-time to my Internet entrepreneur career.

It Wasn't Luck

You may have noticed that I skipped a few details. Like the many hours I devoted to learning and applying everything I could find about Internet marketing and promotion, or the thousands of pages of sales copy I studied to figure out what would and wouldn't work on the Web, or the fact I continued to work with clients as a trainer and coach throughout my years of full-time employment.

What matters is that I learned a lot, and continue to learn, and the whole point of this book is to condense that knowledge into simple, actionable steps that you can follow.

Ryan and his family in Central Park, New York

Getting back to my story:

By mid-2002, my businesses were starting to pay off in a big way. I'd found a model that worked. Through my coaching, I was constantly coming up with new and better ways to help my clients, and I marketed that information in various ways on my websites.

Before long, I was getting as many questions about how to make money as I was about how to get stronger or leaner. I developed products to help my fellow fitness professionals create and market their own products and services online, and by 2007, I had become better known for my entrepreneurial advice than for my fitness knowledge and coaching skill.

Still, there's one thing about my career that drives me a little crazy. I just hate it when people say to me, "Wow! You're really lucky!" It sounds arrogant to point out that luck had nothing to do with my success, so I rarely bother saying it. But I know the truth: I made a plan, I stuck with it, and I worked really hard.

I'd known since I was a little kid that I wanted to be married, have children, and be my own boss. I can even remember thinking how cool it would be to work from home, even though that was long before the Web existed and I had no idea what an adult could actually do that didn't require an office and a staff.

What I didn't know was how I could make any of my plans work. That's why I learned everything I could that I thought would help me. I didn't just study fitness. I also studied marketing, in hopes of figuring out how to create a business from my favorite pursuit.

While my friends and coworkers were at home watching TV, I was at the library or a bookstore, reading everything I could find that might help me succeed. I even read books about success itself, in hopes of finding patterns in other people's success stories that would help me create my own.

I won't say I tried everything I learned. I won't say that everything I tried worked. Some ideas that might've worked for other people won't work for you or me. I made mistakes and hit dead ends. But over time and with experience I figured out what works for most people most of the time. Now I want to show you the best of what I learned.

Meet Your Coach

When I sat down to put together the 21-day Passion to Profit program, I didn't think about it as a book. Instead, I saw it as a coaching program.

Here's what I guarantee: Every business strategy—has been used successfully in the real-world. I've employed all the techniques I recommend for developing products, marketing them, and generating substantial and sustainable revenue from them. They work.

Most important of all, they can change your life. In just 21 days, you'll launch a business that can put you on the road to financial independence.

The 21-Day Program

Instead of filling this book with long-winded theories, I broke everything down into small, specific, easy to understand chunks. After all, even the biggest tree will fall eventually if you take a hard whack at it with an axe every day. Although small, each day's tasks are actionable, and move you closer to your goal. That's how you can create a business in just three weeks.

I've coached and observed enough people to know it's difficult to change ingrained habits in a day, or a week. That's why so many self-help programs, which seem so great the first few days, don't work over the long term.

Each of the 21 days in the Passion to Profit system has its own section, with descriptions of the steps you'll take that day, explanations of why you're taking the steps, and finally a checklist to make sure you have everything covered by the end of the day.

Using the book is easy: Before you start the program, read Chapter 1. I'd also like you to read chapters two through five, but I know that a lot of you will want to jump right into the program. That's okay; I just want you to promise yourself that you'll read the other chapters as you work your way through the program.

Chapter 1

What to Expect While You're Reinventing Yourself

When I sat down to create the Passion to Profit coaching program, I assumed, for the sake of simplicity, that everyone would be starting off at the novice level. But I know that many of you are at different starting points. You could be a complete novice who's never created a product or started a business of any type, or an experienced businessperson who's ready to try something that's more rewarding.

You may be looking to supplement your current income with a part-time endeavor, or ready to jump full-time into a lucrative online business that will provide lifelong income and financial security.

You may not have a clue about what type of product or service you can offer online, or you may have an idea for a business and just need a step-by-step system to get it rolling.

All of you will use the same 21-day program, but no two readers will use it exactly the same way. If you don't have an idea for a product, you'll come up with one, and by the end of the 21 days you'll know exactly what you need to do to produce it and start making money off it. If you have an idea, you can work on it over the next 21 days, and have everything in place to launch it successfully. And if you already have a product, by the end of the 21 days you'll have that product in the marketplace and generating revenue for you.

In fact, you can even do the 21-day program twice. The first time, you'll come up with the idea for a product or business and figure out how you're going to produce it and earn money. The second time, you'll launch your new business and start making money. Ready? Let's get started.

Chapter 2

Everything You Need for a Spectacular Life

Ryan and his son Jake

Let's begin by defining the word success. I came across a version of this definition by Jack Canfield and it resonated so strongly that I quickly adapted it for myself:

"To have the freedom to do what I want, when I want, as often as I want"

Success is freedom. Financial freedom. Being free from illness, sickness, or pain. Having unlimited free time. Which is nice to know, but it still begs the question: How do we get there?

Change Your Attitude and Your Behaviors Will Follow

Most self-help advice, in my view, is a Band Aid. It helps you stop the bleeding, but it doesn't heal the wound. It might even make things worse, in the same way a wound that's been poorly treated can get infected.

Here's what I mean: Let's say you're unemployed, broke, and sliding into debt. You get a job, so you're no longer unemployed. You've applied a Band Aid, and stopped the bleeding. But, have you fixed the problem that left you unemployed in the first place?

We've all heard of lottery winners who become multimillionaires overnight, but somehow manage to lose all the money and end up right back where they were.

The lottery winner might blame it on bad investments, greedy family members, or duplicitous advisors. My take is that he's pointing the finger of blame in the wrong direction. His financial thermostat was set on "low." When money dropped into his life, the thermostat temporarily reset itself to "high," but that was so far outside his comfort level that he allowed himself to make a series of errors and miscalculations until it returned to where it was before.

Why would he do this? Well, put yourself in his place. Would you be comfortable with lots of money? Before you answer, ask yourself if you've ever described a wealthy person with phrases like "filthy rich," "greedy bastard," or "pretentious snob." The person in question may have deserved your scorn, but you also have to consider the possibility that you're uncomfortable with the idea of wealth, that you have a thought process that assumes large sums of money can't be made honestly or ethically. You aren't alone if you think that way. Movies and television routinely depict rich people in the worst possible way. From Gilligan's Island to Titanic, you see wealthy characters who're at best clueless, and at worst cruel, selfish, underhanded, and hateful.

The person I've just described suffers from a serious problem: negativity. I understand that there could be serious physical or mental health issues underlying a negative outlook; in those cases, of course I recommend medical help. But most people I talk to in my work suffer from what you could call self-inflicted negativity. They've developed a toxic, corrosive attitude toward success without even realizing it.

Getting Rid of Negativity

A lot of forces work against you in our society. Unhappy people inflict you with their negative thoughts wherever you go. If you were to approach this as an observer, rather than a participant, you'd be shocked at the sheer pervasiveness of negativity each of us encounters on an hourly basis. You can't change the tone, but you can choose to ignore it. It wasn't easy, but I taught myself to do exactly that. You can, too, by following this five-step plan:

Step 1: End Your Media Addiction

I don't have a 21-day program to accomplish this. I think the best approach is to cut off the media all at once. Cold turkey. Stop watching the news during the 21 days of the Passion to Profit program. Stop reading the newspaper. Most of all, stop listening to political talk shows on AM radio and stop watching the shout fests on TV.

I know what you are thinking. "If I stop watching the news or reading the paper, how will I know when something important happens?" Trust me on this: If something important happens, you'll know. It'll be impossible to avoid. You'll see it in an email, or get a text message on your cell phone, or just overhear it in a conversation. I haven't watched the news or read a newspaper regularly for more than three years, and I have yet to miss out on something important. I know if there's a snowstorm coming (not an unimportant detail in my life, considering that I live in Connecticut). I know when there's an election. I'm not saying you should forego your rights and duties as a citizen by not voting, or by remaining ignorant of the important issues in your part of the world. You can selectively find and absorb the information you really need without subjecting yourself to everything else.

You know what I mean by "everything else." How much information do you really need about the woman who just drowned her three helpless children? Like I said, you can't avoid knowing that it happened. You'll come across the basic facts even if you're trying to avoid them. What you don't need, and what you can avoid, are the minor details about her life that trickle out day after day, or the endless sermonizing about why it happened.

I'm sure you know people who get sucked into these big media sensations—the O.J. Simpson trial, the Michael Jackson death, the never-ending saga of Britney Spears. You and I both know people who ended up spending hours every day following these stories. Honestly, can you think of any reason why anyone would make such a thing a priority in life?

Every now and then I revert to old habits. Not long ago, I listened to a radio talk show for a few minutes. The big news story of the day was that a major investment-banking firm, which had a great year, had announced its annual bonuses. The average employee at the firm was set to receive something like $300,000, which of course is a nice chunk of change. I mean, who wouldn't want to get a check like that, on top of a regular salary that's pretty good to begin with? When I heard the news, my first thought was, "Good for them!" I assumed they played by the rules, worked hard, and exceeded whatever expectations their employer and clients had for them. To me, it's like a pro athlete who has a great year and then scores a major raise in his next contract. It's about performance, and he performed.

But you'd never guess that the employees of that firm might've earned the money. The hosts of the show seemed outraged over the size of the bonuses, and the listeners who called in, if anything, were even more upset. So I began to think about what the recipients of those bonuses would do with the money. Let's put you in that situation. It's bonus time, and you've just gotten a check for $300,000. And let's say that, after taxes, there was enough left over for you to fulfill a dream of yours and buy a bigger, nicer house for your family. Your bonus becomes the down payment for that house.

Who benefits, besides you and your family? First, of course, is the family that's selling the house to you. Maybe they want to move up to a bigger house, or downsize to a smaller place, or need to move to another part of the country because of a job change. Your bonus has certainly helped them. The real-estate agents on both sides of the deal receive commissions, as does the mortgage broker. Attorneys and house inspectors get paid.

You also sell your current house, which means a dream fulfilled for the family that buys it. The Realtors and brokers and inspectors again get their share. So do three different sets of movers—one each for your family, the family you're buying from, and the family you're selling to. If you've ever bought or sold a home, you know that inevitably you and the buyers and sellers make repairs and upgrades and cosmetic changes. That means carpenters, painters, landscapers, roofers, and who knows how many specialists in flooring and windows and plumbing get paid for their work. So do the people who make and sell the materials. So do the people who make and sell you new furniture or appliances or whatever else you need in your new home.

Then there are the taxes you pay on all these transactions. You pay for schools, roads, libraries, recreation programs, police, firemen, administrators… and that's just the local taxes. You've also paid state and federal taxes on the original $300,000 bonus. Now, if you were the recipient of that $300,000 bonus, knew that you'd earned it for honest work you performed, and knew that so many people and institutions had profited from it, wouldn't it surprise you to know that complete strangers were complaining about it on a radio show?

How bizarre is that?

Here's my challenge to you. For the next three weeks, do everything you can to avoid news in any form—TV, talk radio, newspapers. You won't believe how liberating it is.

Step 2: Beware of Energy-Sucking Vampires

When I worked at the children's hospital, I had lunch every day with five guys from the maintenance department. They worked all over the hospital, fixing everything from the lights to the medical equipment. They were fun to hang around with, but they were also overwhelmingly negative. They could find something bad to say about any person or situation. Moreover, they were proud of this peculiar talent, and happy to share their thoughts and observations with everyone they encountered. After three months, I just couldn't take the negativity anymore. Even then, as a 23-year-old, I knew it wasn't good for my psyche. I could feel the energy and enthusiasm leaving my body like air from a punctured tire every time I was around them.

I didn't need to confront them, or create any drama. I figured it's better to be alone than surrounded by negative people, so I started going out for lunch by myself. I'd grab a quick bite, then head to the local Barnes & Noble to read for 20 minutes. It was a double-duty upgrade in my life: Not only had I gotten rid of a big source of negativity, I was using the time productively, to move my life and career forward.

Step 3: Drive and Grow Rich

If you've followed steps 1 and 2, you have some extra time on your hands. Now it's time to fill it in a positive, productive way. Let's start with one situation in which most of us are captive to negativity: our commute to and from work. The average person commutes 30 minutes each way. That's an hour a day, five hours a week, 20 hours a month, and more than 200 hours a year.

I highly recommend listening to audio books or motivational programs. You can learn more in an hour with a well-chosen audio book than you could in a month of listening to AM radio ranting. Plus, as a bonus, you'll never have to listen to a commercial.

Now, with one simple change, you've replaced the random

negativity of broadcast media with positive, progressive steps toward improving your mind and your outlook.

If you look in my car, you'll find dozens of audio programs. I really like the motivational programs by Brian Tracy, Jack Canfield, and Anthony Robbins, among others. I genuinely enjoy listening to them. In fact, I might be the only guy in America who looks forward to a 20-hour drive from Connecticut to Florida with four small children in the car. I see it as 20 hours of information and insight I can absorb. (I should note that this strategy is flexible. More often than not, I'll listen to my programs on an iPod while my wife listens to the radio or reads to the kids. But if we feel like talking, we talk.)

Step 4: Be SMART

If you want to reach your full potential, you must set goals. A great acronym for goal setting is SMART:

Specific: Be as detailed and specific as you can with your goals. Instead of saying, "I want to be fit," you can say, "I want to lose 12 pounds of body fat in 12 months by working out for at least 12 minutes a day, 5 days a week."

Measurable: You must be able to measure your results. For example, instead of saying, "I want to be really rich," your goal can be stated as, "I want to be free of debt and have $500,000 in my bank account within 36 months."

Attainable: Is your goal within your reach? Wanting to become a millionaire might be an attainable goal for you, but is it attainable within the time frame you've allotted?

Relevant: Is your goal relevant towards your life purpose? Think long and hard about what you feel you're on earth to do. Does your goal bring you closer or farther away from your purpose?

Time-Based: Your goal should have a deadline. Never leave it open ended and pick a specific date you will reach your goal.

If your goals aren't SMART, they're really just daydreams. But if they are SMART, you can run every significant decision through a simple filter:

"Is this action bringing me closer to my goals, is it a distraction from my goals, or is it just something that keeps me where I am right now?"

Step 5: Take Control of Your Life and Keep Control

After you've gotten rid of negative influences and gotten SMART about your goals, it's time to work on the final obstacle to your success: you. You must take responsibility for everything in your life. And I mean everything.

You have to give yourself credit for your successes and take the blame for your failures. You have to acknowledge that both are the products of your actions, or lack of action.

If you're unhappy with your job or the size of your bank accounts, you need to take responsibility for that. Don't blame the economy. Blame yourself.

Sometimes—and I'll admit this is a tricky area—it helps to take responsibility for things that may legitimately be out of your control. Bad genes happen to good people. I don't want you to beat yourself up over things that nobody in his right mind would blame on you. But I will say this: Blaming and buck-passing are corrosive. Taking responsibility is a liberating feeling. That's why, in my experience, it frees your mind and unleashes your creative spirit to take complete responsibility for everything in your life.

Five Bonus Tips

These tips aren't part of the program, but I've found them tremendously helpful on the path to success. (For even more tips, be sure to checkout my blog at <u>ryanlee.com</u>.)

Participate in a Mastermind group: Find a group of four or five like-minded people, people who share your ambitions and attitudes toward success. Commit to meet on the phone at least once a month. You not only get to bounce your own ideas off your peers, you help them move toward their goals.

Act "as if": Imagine you've already achieved your dreams. When you act "as if" you've followed through on your plans and reached your goals, you often get insight into how to achieve those goals. If your business plan had already succeeded and made you wealthy and influential in your field, what would you say to a writer during an interview for a local newspaper? If you were a speaker at a seminar, how would you address an audience of people who want to know how you got from where they are to where you are now?

Remember that money loves speed: Don't procrastinate. I have one acquaintance who has been working on the same Internet project for almost four years. When you have an idea, take immediate action. Napoleon Hill once said, "Don't wait. The time will never be just right."

Double your output: The best time-management tip I've even come across is this: Stop checking email so often. If you have an alert that lets you know when a new email has arrived, turn it off. Set specific times during the day when you'll check email. Here's the second-best, time saving tip: Put tasks together into chunks. Returning phone calls can be a chunk—instead of returning them piecemeal, return them all in the same block of time. "Chunk" your bills by paying all of them at the same time, rather than one at a time. Even if you pay some earlier than they need to be paid, you'll still come out ahead because you've used your time more efficiently.

Outsource: Is there a part of your business that you don't like, or aren't particularly good at? Can you hire someone else to do it? It pays to outsource back-office tasks like billing or customer support, rather than taking them on yourself and running the risk that you'll procrastinate or do them poorly. Think of it this way: When was the last time you changed the oil on your own car? Or repaired your own computer? You could probably learn to do those things, but you probably decided long ago that it made more sense to pay someone else to do it, someone who could do it quickly and efficiently. Now extend that attitude to your business.

One Final Thought

My goal with the detox program and the bonus tips is to help you cut through all the noise and clutter of modern life, and by doing so take control of your life. Most of you should be able to act on these tips. But, as I mentioned earlier in the chapter, some of you will need professional help. (Remember, I'm married to a psychologist.) If you have serious, deep-rooted issues, and feel as if you're always getting stuck in the same rut, please seek the advice of a qualified counselor or therapist. I truly want to help you get the most out of life. If you aren't able to act on all the steps of my coaching program, it won't work.

Chapter 3

How to Create a 24-Hour-a-Day, Seven-Day-a-Week Cash Machine

I'm not a financial guru, I don't have an Ivy League MBA, and I've never worked as a financial planner. What I have is real-world experience. I've built a handful of successful businesses on the Internet with start-up costs of less than $100 per venture. If I wanted to, I could stop working today and live comfortably off the income from those businesses for the rest of my life.

I'm not knocking higher education. I have a master's degree in exercise physiology, which has helped me become a better trainer and coach. I'm married to a woman with a Ph.D. in her field, as I've mentioned. But, if you have any notion that you need specialized education or training in business or finance to succeed as an entrepreneur, I want to convince you otherwise.

Here's a story from my own graduate studies that helps illustrate my point:

I went to night school for three years to earn my master's degree. As my time in the program was coming to a close, I had an interesting conversation with my exercise physiology professor.

By that time, I was already generating income selling coaching programs and information products on the Internet. My professor, as it happens, had recently produced his own DVD, but he'd lost money on the deal. And here he was asking me for advice after class.

My professor, of course, was an expert in exercise science, not finance. Still, I was surprised that he hadn't done any research into marketing before he produced and tried to sell his product.

That's when I realized that if I wanted to make more money, I'd have to seek out the people who've done what I wanted to do. I'd have to buy their programs, attend their seminars, perhaps even hire them to coach me. In other words, I needed to stop modeling unsuccessful people, and study the ones who've done what I wanted to do.

Boy, did it work.

I've gone from a recreational therapist making $26,000 a year and living in my parents' basement to a millionaire. I did it by studying other successful people and taking immediate action on my ideas.

My Big Discovery: It's Not What You Make, It's What You Keep

At the time of that discussion with my professor, I approached income and employment the way most people do. I concentrated on my full-time job and I made extra money by trading hours for dollars as a personal trainer. I made money when I worked. I didn't make money when I wasn't working—when I was eating, sleeping, studying for my master's degree, or spending time with my wife. Like almost everyone else, my potential to make money was limited by the number of hours I could work and the amount of money I could persuade other people to pay me.

In one of my grad-school classes, the assignment was to plan out a business we'd like to run. At the time, I wanted to open a personal-training studio. So I did the required research, visited a few facilities, and ran the numbers.

Those numbers told me the business didn't make much sense.

Start-up costs would be $50,000 to $100,000, and that was for a small studio. A bigger, more ambitious set-up could cost millions—all before I'd signed up a single member or trained a single client.

It would take years for a commercial gym or personal-training studio to turn a profit, and there was no guarantee it would ever happen. Even in successful gyms, the margins were razor-thin; a few clients flaking out, an unexpected lawsuit, or some other random instance of bad luck could mean the difference between black ink and red. And that was if you did everything right. Make a few mistakes, as all entry-level business people will do, and you could lose every penny of your investment, leaving you with a stack of unpaid bills that might take years to pay off.

At the time I was taking the class and doing this research, I'd already launched my first Internet business for less than $50. I wasn't getting rich, but I'd been operating in the black from the first week.

You don't need an MBA or a Ph.D. in statistics to see how important it is to keep overhead as low as possible. I ran the business by myself from my home, so I didn't have to pay anybody or take on the burden of a lease. In fact, I didn't have any employees for my first four years in business. So I dropped the fantasy of having my own training facility. I learned more about information marketing, and realized that it really is the perfect business. Here's why:

I can work from anywhere. I started my first Internet business from my parents' basement. Now, with a wireless modem, I can write information products by the pool, or answer emails from a bookstore. I can travel almost anywhere in the world and run my businesses from any place with Internet access. Wherever I am, there's my office.

I can launch new businesses with almost no costs. All I need is an idea, a URL, and a mailing list. If I produce a good product or offer a good service, I make money. If the idea or my execution of it misfires, I can learn from my mistake and move on to the next idea without sacrificing any of the money I've earned from the ideas that worked.

My business can be run with zero headaches. There's no need to deal with full-time employees, and the headaches that come with running a fully staffed office. You can outsource all of the day-to-day tasks to "work for hire" companies.

My customers can buy my products and services no matter where they live, as I realized back in 1999, when I got an email from the United Kingdom. Someone in London was asking me questions about training. I found that mind-boggling. If I'd opened that training studio, I'd be limited to clients who lived within driving distance. Today, I have customers in 32 different countries.

Once I have a product or service that works—that was well-conceived, well-executed, and well-marketed—I can make money from that product 24 hours a day, seven days a week. There is no limit to the amount of money I can generate from a single product. And there's no limit to the number of businesses I can run simultaneously.

You Too Can Play This Game

As I said in the preface to Passion to Profit, I don't have any special genius that allows me to run my businesses with low overhead and big returns. You can produce a downloadable book that costs you virtually nothing beyond your time and effort. You can charge whatever you think your target audience is willing to pay—$5, $100, or anything in between. That's with no office expenses, no employees, no inventory, and no fulfillment costs. Almost every penny you make is profit. Turn the page, and I'll show you how.

How to Turn Your Knowledge, Skills or Hobbies into Money - Lots and Lots of Money

At this point, I wouldn't blame you if you entertained the thought that I might not be completely sane. We've all been conditioned to look at our knowledge, skills, and interests as commodities we can rent out to a finite number of clients in a circumscribed geographic area. We see our best assets as having limited worth, because they're of limited value to our employer or clients. They're worth whatever this small circle of people says they're worth.

But I can promise you this: You know something that other people don't. Everyone has some type of specialized information, or has a talent for finding specialized information, that other people want and are willing to purchase. I've spoken with thousands of people who wanted to know more about creating information products, and I've yet to meet anyone who had nothing to offer. There's always something you can turn into an information product.

About a year before I wrote this chapter, my wife and I attended a wedding in upstate Connecticut. A guy at our table told us he installs car stereos for a living. He works two jobs to support his family, which includes a newborn son. My first thought was, this guy could make some terrific information products. I could see him creating a series of DVDs teaching people how to do it themselves. Or publishing a private newsletter for industry technicians, where they could share news about what they do, and strategies for doing it better or more profitably. My second thought was, he could make enough money off these products that he wouldn't need to work that second job. Maybe he could do so well that he wouldn't need the first job. I've seen it happen more times than I could ever count.

Here are some more examples of how you can profit from the information you already have. I'm going to use extremely specific examples, but each one applies to a broad range of similar jobs. The suggestions I offer for an electronics salesman who specializes in home-theater equipment could apply to any type of salesman with a specialty. Similarly, anybody who builds or repairs things—from electricians to pastry chefs—should be able to use variations on the suggestions I make for a handyman in the second example.

Electronics salesperson

Let's say you work the floor at a big electronics retailer. The store sells everything from cell phones to high-definition televisions, but you've developed a specialty in home theaters. You're good at selling them. And because you've been dealing with the public for a long time, you've started to see some patterns in the types of questions they ask and the concerns they express. So your first option for an information product could be something that helps these consumers.

Topic 1: "How to set up and get the most out of your new home theater"

Market: people who buy sophisticated audio and video equipment, but don't understand how it works and quickly become frustrated with the products and their own inability to use them in a way that justifies the money they've spent

What they want: to learn how to set up the home theater; to get the most out of it once it's set up properly; and to be able to trouble-shoot the problems that inevitably arise

Potential information products: manuals, DVDs, e-books

Yes, the products themselves come with installation manuals. And there's no shortage of magazines and books for electronics aficionados who're always looking for the latest, greatest stuff. But think about your own experience with owner's manuals. Are they simple, clear, and easy to use? Maybe you understand what they're trying to say, but chances are your customers find them infuriating. Now think about the products that appeal to audio and video buffs. Aren't they way over the head of the average consumer, the person who's mystified by the instruction booklet?

So you see a potential gap in the information marketplace. The person who isn't handy, who doesn't have an intuitive feel for electronics, gets little from the existing material. The product that speaks directly to that person and addresses his most pressing concerns probably doesn't yet exist, and won't exist until you create it.

But maybe you're more interested in helping your fellow salespeople than you are in addressing the concerns of your customers. In that case…

Topic 2: "How to improve your sales of big-ticket electronics by 50 percent"

Market: store managers, commission-based salespeople

What they want: to improve sales

Potential information products: audio CDs (which they can listen to on the way to work), workbooks, seminars

Again, there's lots of material about how to understand consumers and how to be a better salesman. You should already be familiar with it. But is there a book or product that specifically addresses people like you, who make a living selling a specific type of product? If not, you could be the one to create it.

I put seminars on the list of potential products. If you're a good salesman, you're probably a good public speaker. And people in your profession probably respond to person-to-person instruction better than textbooks. So this is a great opportunity to hit the road and speak to groups of salespeople. In most cases, their employers will pay for them to attend your seminars, since the employers have the most to gain.

One last audience to consider: people who want to purchase the type of products you sell but are fearful of the process.

This person probably wants something short, simple, straightforward, and up to date. (The beauty of products like e-books, which I'll discuss in more detail at the end of this chapter, is that they can be updated constantly without leaving you with a garage full of obsolete books or pamphlets.)

Since this customer fears people like you, you'll give her courage in the form of a product that reveals all the dirty tricks of your profession. And yes, your profession has dirty tricks; every trade does. I'm a trainer, and I could tell you stories about people in my field that would give you nightmares.

She needs simple guidelines that help her narrow her choices, so tell her how much power she needs for the space she has, what types of optional equipment improve the picture or sound, what stuff is useless but will get pushed at her anyway, and how much money she should expect to spend.

There's also information that would be helpful but that she wouldn't think to seek out. So tell her the best time of year to buy these products, what brands have better track records than others, and what "code words" she can use to tip off a salesperson that she isn't an easy mark for unscrupulous tactics.

You may need to do this type of product anonymously, so you don't jeopardize your current job. In fact, anonymity could give the product more value, since it tells your customer that she's getting information so valuable, and so closely guarded, that you'd get fired if your boss found out you were spilling the secrets only insiders are supposed to know.

Handyman

As someone with a broad background in repairing all the things that break, you have an easy and natural transition into information products. Fewer homeowners these days know how to fix anything; our natural inclination is to panic the minute something starts to creak, leak, or crack. So you have two big market opportunities: people who want to learn how to do it themselves, and people who are good with their hands and want to get into the business you're already in.

Home Depot and Lowe's have shelves full of books on home repair, and offer seminars for homeowners. So what can you do that they can't? You can explain how to do the work faster, or with less expense. You can show insider's secrets and shortcuts. You can appeal to new-home buyers by showing simple and inexpensive ways to make their home more functional, or go the other direction and show people trying to sell a home how to make it appear more cozy or luxurious.

Topic 1: "How to quickly and easily fix your own ..."

Market: homeowners who can't afford to hire someone every time something snaps; homeowners who can afford it but don't want to pay someone out of principle; entry-level landlords who own a small number of rental properties and whose profit margins disappear every time they have to call a professional to fix something a tenant has broken; people who live out in the middle of nowhere and have a hard time getting anyone to come out for minor household work

What they want: to save money on basic household repairs, and to feel empowered with the knowledge that they can fix things

Potential information products: how-to manuals; DVDs; seminars

The key here is to use your personal experiences as a handyman to understand what people want that they can't get from the materials that already exist. Are they looking for projects that improve home value? Increase storage space? Allow them to heat or cool their homes with less energy? Just about any concern a client expresses to you could be the basis for an information product.

Whatever information product you start off with should work to your strengths. If you're good at articulating your ideas and explaining how to make them work, then you'll probably be able to produce useful how-to manuals and be comfortable speaking at your seminars. Are you a natural teacher? Consider offering workshops. If you're more comfortable doing than explaining, DVDs would probably work best for you.

Topic 2: "How to make money as a handyman"

Market: people who enjoy fixing and improving things and want to know how to make a living at it; people who already have a full-time job and are looking for a way to earn part-time income

What they want: straightforward, actionable information on how to go from being good with their hands to making money doing what they enjoy

Potential information products: how-to manuals; DVDs; seminars and workshops

How to Make Money from Your Hobbies

By now, you might be thinking that the two examples I offered don't have anything to do with you. You aren't a talented, experienced salesperson with a lucrative specialty. You aren't someone who has the skills of a handyman. Maybe you've bounced around from job to job and don't think you have any specialized knowledge or talent that you can teach others.

Get that thought out of your head. There's always something you know or can do better than other people. *Always.*

If your profession offers no obvious possibilities, look at your hobbies.

What do you like to do? Put another way: When you're at work, what do you wish you could be doing instead? What do you most look forward to doing outside of work? What do you love to talk about when you're out with friends and family? What topic can you go on and on about for hours? In what area of knowledge do people who know you come to you for advice?

Maybe you love to shop. If so, you've probably learned a lot about shopping without realizing it. You can teach others where to find the most valuable coupons, when retailers have their best sales of the year for a variety of categories (clothes, cars, electronics), or how to find second-hand shops that offer the highest-quality, least-used stuff that other people bought but didn't bother taking out of the box. Because you love to shop, you've figured out how to get bargains that are invisible to almost everyone else. That means you can create an information product that shows other shoppers what only the truly obsessed shoppers would know or could easily find out.

Let's say you're a fashion buff. You spend your free time flipping through fashion magazines, and challenge yourself to recreate those looks for a fraction of the price. Sometimes you find ways to improve on what you see in the magazines. Your friends come to you for advice on what to wear and how to wear it. It doesn't matter if you're an intern or a CEO—if you have this kind of fashion sense, and you gained it despite the fact no one paid you to have it, you can create information products. You can teach people how to dress better than they do now— which fabrics and patterns look good together, and which should never be seen on the same body at the same time. You can help people with different body types find clothes that fit better and are more flattering. No, you aren't a big-name designer or a buyer for a major department-store chain or a writer for Vogue or GQ. But, you probably have a better grasp on the sartorial dilemmas of people like you than the highly paid, highly visible fashion elite.

Or you could mix and match within these two categories, and exploit specialties within specialties. Maybe you're an obsessed shopper who's particularly obsessed with fashion. Or you're a fashion hound who's particularly good with children's outfits. If you love it, you're good at it, and your friends ask for your advice about it, you can create an information product on that topic.

Some more general topic areas where you might have some expertise:

Academics (standardized-test prep; how to get into a specific college or type of college; best preschools for a variety of incomes and preferences; guides to tutors who live in your area)

Athletics (sports skills; coaching; sport-specific conditioning; best schools and camps to improve sports skills)

Collectibles (how to become a collector with a particular specialty, such as baseball cards, stamps, coins, or antiques; how to sell a collection you inherited; how to buy or sell collectibles on eBay without getting ripped off)

Computer skills (Internet search tips and tricks; creating websites; getting more hits on your blog; computer repair and maintenance; salvaging information from old machines; mastering specific programs for specific purposes—"PowerPoint for high school teachers," for example)

Cooking (finding, sharing or creating recipes; mastering techniques; shopping for exotic ingredients; making everyday comfort food taste like haute cuisine)

Decorating (interior design; party themes; shopping for unusual and eclectic objects)

Exercise (weight loss; aesthetics; sports performance; getting started; sticking with a long-term program)

Language skills (master or teach a second language; learn just enough of a language to make travel in a foreign country more enjoyable; improve vocabulary; learn better ways to explain concepts; become a better conversationalist)

Martial arts (basic skills; real-world self-defense; teaching martial arts to kids with special needs)

Musical instruments (how to tune or repair them; how to buy one new or used; how to teach others to play them; how to restore antique instruments)

Parenting (dealing with difficult teens; surviving as a single parent; helping mixed-race or mixed-religion families cope; shopping for the best bargains in strollers, cribs and other baby gear)

Regional interests (reviews of area restaurants; best stores in a variety of categories; how to find the best contractors or doctors or other professionals in your area; shortcuts for commuters)

Travel (the best places to stay; how to save money while traveling; how to save money for traveling; everything a traveler would want to know about a particular place)

Video games (winning at specific games or types of games; buying and selling; learning cheat codes; finding rare vintage games; troubleshooting specific game systems)

You don't have to be the best in the world in any of these areas, or any other areas in which you have an interest. You just have to be more knowledgeable, skilled, or experienced than the person buying your product.

Now, having said that, I don't want you to misinterpret my words and think you can sell products with inaccurate or useless information, or pedestrian tips that your customer could find in a few seconds with a simple Google search.

You must be able to deliver whatever you've promised to deliver, for two big reasons:

1. Ethics. If you're taking the customer's money, you have to make a sincere effort to give that customer the best and most useful information you can deliver.

2. Profit. A customer who feels burned by your first product will never buy your next product. It's much harder to find a new customer than it is to sell a follow-up product to an existing client.

In other words, you must deliver value. But, that's true of any job in which you're being compensated. If you work for someone else, you know that your boss will fire you if your work doesn't rise to the value of your compensation, in his judgment. If you work for yourself by creating and selling information products, your customers will fire you if your products don't deliver what they expect for the price they've paid.

Chapter 4

The Producer Model

How to Create an Information Product, Even if You Have No Skills or Specialized Knowledge

Let's say you're interested in a particular topic, but don't feel as if you have the knowledge, skill, and experience to produce a valuable information product. You can still make money from your area of interest by following the "producer model".

Think about what a producer does in Hollywood.

They organize the project: everything from hiring the director and choosing the cast to raising the money. But, with that responsibility comes a lion share of the profits too.

Sure, the talent (movie stars) receive the adoration of millions of fans, however it's the producer that makes the big money when they have a hit. So if you don't mind being in shadows, you can still make a really nice online income behind the scenes.

Interview Other Experts

Maybe you're interested in leadership training, but you know you're at the front end of the learning process. You aren't yet a leader or someone who can train leaders. But, you're fascinated by the subject and want to know more.

You can create an information product now—as in, starting today—by making a list of the experts in this area, the people you admire and hope to emulate. Include some people who've written about leadership, as well as people who in your estimation are great leaders in their professions or avocations. Find some big names in the field, but also some people who aren't as well known.

Google them and get their contact information.

Now ask each one if you can conduct an interview for your upcoming project. Successful people love to share their expertise and wisdom with others. Their time is valuable, of course, but you'd be surprised at how accommodating they can be. Make sure to let them know you'll be recording the interview, and that you'll include it in a product you're selling—a book, audio program, newsletter, or whatever it is. You'll want to get their written permission to use this information, or at least an email in which it's clear they understand and agree to participate in your project. Once you have a handful of these interviews on tape— how many you need depends on the length and quality of the interviews—you can sell them as an audio CD, a series of CDs, or downloadable audio mp3 files.

You can also transcribe the interviews (or pay to have them transcribed), edit the transcripts, and sell the collection as a book, manual, or series of downloadable text files. Or you can do both: Package the audio CDs with the written transcripts and offer it as a multimedia package. If the information and insights contained in the interviews are really good, useful, and not obvious or well known, you have a product that can sell for a premium price—$100, $400, maybe even more.

I created a compilation program called Speed Experts (speedexperts.com). I asked 18 different strength coaches to create a 30-day speed-training program. Altogether, the programs comprise more than 800 downloadable pages. It sells for $97 online.

A student of mine, Virgil Aponte, borrowed this idea and did the same thing for improving vertical jump (jumpexperts.net). Another student, Jen Heath, took this concept for fat loss and created The Fat Loss Pros.

Expert Compensation

Before you start to shout and say, "Hey Ryan, are you crazy? I don't have thousands of dollars to pay these experts for interviews!", I want to let you in on a little secret.

These experts will do the interviews for free. Yes, for free.

Why on earth would an expert agree to be interviewed for free?

For exposure and publicity. The smart experts know the more people that hear them, the more of their own products they will sell. Yes, the smart experts also have their own information products (books, home study kits, seminars, etc.).

Just make sure you let them know the interview will be recorded and sold. A simple email agreement is just fine.

I've literally interviewed over 500 experts over the past 10+ years, and only one time did someone ask to be compensated for the interview. And I politely declined.

And before I forget, you will have experts either decline to be interviewed or never give the courtesy of an email reply. And that's ok too. Just move on to the next person on your list.

The key is getting the first person. Once you get that first "yes", ask if they know any other experts in the field that would be a good candidate for the interview. More than likely, they are well connected and are happy to introduce you to others.

Then the ball really gets rolling and you are on your way to the producer riches!

A Business You Can Run on Autopilot

By the time you finish reading Passion to Profit you'll have dozens of ideas for different information products you can create. But, for the purposes of the 21-day coaching program, I want you to think about one particular type of product: an **e-book**.

An e-book can be as short and simple as a 50-page report sold as a PDF file, or as big and complex as you want to make it, with the caveat that whatever you produce can be downloaded by your customers.

I'm known in the "Internet marketing circles" as the 'membership guy'. And believe me, I love membership sites and any business that brings in recurring revenue. But it's not always the best choice as your first product.

Here's why I think an e-book is the perfect inaugural product:

No inventory. Customers purchase your product and download it to their computers. You can turn a profit from the very first sale, and use your profits for marketing this product or creating new ones.

No printing. If your customers want a printed copy, they'll use their own equipment. That saves you time and money.

Nothing to ship. Fulfillment is automatic—once the customer has paid for and downloaded the product, the transaction is complete. You don't have to worry about buying envelopes, printing mailing labels, and making daily runs to the post office.

No inventory. Printing books are a thing of the past. Once you upload your file to the Internet, you're done. No more garages full of unsold books and products.

No limit to your sales. A digital product can be sold an infinite number of times to as many customers as you can generate. That means there's no limit to the amount of money you can make on a single product, or a line of products.

Always updated. If you need to update your information, just make the changes and upload the new file. It takes just minutes and your customers now have the freshest information on your topic.

No barrier to entry. Like I've been saying, anyone can get into the business of producing and selling information products. It's not like getting into Harvard or running for office. Entrepreneurs are self-selected.

No need for you to be present. Once you've created and set up the mechanism for selling the product, it's always on sale. Anyone with a credit card and Internet access can buy it. You can be anywhere, doing anything, and never have to worry about sales and fulfillment.

I hope you're excited about the idea of getting into this business. I'm looking forward to showing you exactly how to do it.

If you're ready, let's get started.

Chapter 5

Your 21-Day Passion to Profit Coaching Program

Over the next 21 days, I'll be your personal business and success coach. I'll give you a template to help you launch your new career as an online entrepreneur. The program is based on the same principles I've taught clients who paid me up to $1,000 an hour to teach them.

If you want to see real results, you just have to follow three rules:

- Start on Day 1
- Do everything recommended for each day but no more than that (in other words, don't get ahead of yourself and try to do two days at once)
- Follow the program in order until you finish Day 21

The coaching system depends on progressions to work. Each step you complete laying the groundwork for the next step. Think of it this way: if you were building a house, and tried to construct a frame on a concrete foundation that hadn't yet dried, what would happen? You'd be surprised how many new businesses fail for similar reasons.

The Two Approaches

Chances are you fall into one of two categories.

1. You already know exactly what you'd like to do, the type of product you want to create, and the market you're going to reach.

2. You have no idea what you want to do.

If you're in category #2, you may not be able to complete each step in a single day. It's entirely possible to create a product in 21 days, while simultaneously developing a mailing list and marketing plan, but ultimately it depends on the amount and depth of information you plan to include. Many products can't be written and produced on that timetable. Even if your goal is a shorter, more tightly focused product, you may not be able to work that fast.

That means some of you will need more than a day on some steps. That's okay; just stick to the order and take the time you need to complete each step.

Conversely, if you already have a product, you won't need an entire day for some of the steps. That's fine, too. You can move ahead, as long as you do all of the steps, and do them in order.

If you're in category #2, you can use the 21-day coaching program as a step-by-step introduction to the principles of product creation and marketing. I'm still going to ask you to "create" a product, but more as an exercise than as a business that you'll have launched by the end of the 21 days. In some parts of the program, the instructions will be more contemplative than actionable—you'll think about what you'd do at this stage, and perform some background research, rather than actually doing it. You could look at it as a practice run. When you're sure of the product you want to create, you can start over at any time and repeat the 21 steps—this time with the goal of launching a real business with real revenue.

Your "Take Action" Checklists

After coaching thousands of people to success, I've found it's best to break large goals into small, easily attainable tasks. That's why I've summarized all your assignments for each day, and put them into checklist form. Simply check off each assignment when you complete it. If you have to travel or have to take off for any other reason, don't sweat it. Just take the day off. When you get back, continue where you left off.

By the end of the 21 days, you can expect measurable improvements. Some of you may actually have an information product for sale and generating revenue three weeks from now. Remember, this program is just the beginning of your journey. I have more resources and programs for you at ryanlee.com.

Day 1:
Choose Your Target Market and Topic

Your Market

If you were to disregard everything else I tell you about creating a profitable business, I hope you'll pay attention to this: Your first step, before you do anything else, is to identify your audience. Before you build a website, write an e-book, or create a blog, you must know who your website, e-book or blog is for.

You need to know exactly who your customer is and why they'd be interested in your product, and if they have the money to buy it.

Please don't make the mistake of the newbie marketer and say you want to sell to "everyone". If you're trying to sell to everyone, you'll end up selling to no one.

In order to streamline your marketing and define your vision, you have to narrow down your target market. This way you'll know exactly what they want and how you can reach them directly.

The number one mistake new marketers make when they start their online business is to not spend enough time doing research on their market. There are two ways to narrow down your potential audience in a definitive way: demographics and psychographics.

Demographics:
Demographics are quantifiable characteristics of your customer base. For example: age, gender, race, geographic location, income, religion, political or professional affiliations or whatever else is a

measurable, identifiable trait of your potential audience.

Psychographics:
These characteristics are more subtle than demographics. What do they care about? What do they value? What are they afraid of? What pushes their buttons and moves them to action? This can be a way to characterize them as well.

Look at your product and service and decide what type of demographic or psychographic characteristics your ideal customers share. For example, if you are selling an e-book on dating as a Christian, your target market will obviously be religious and single. If you are selling a video course on setting up your own home security system, your target market will have the common psychographic element, which will be the desire to maintain safety in one's home.

Brainstorm a list of characteristics of your target market. Who will be most likely to buy your product and what do they have in common? This list will become more important in the coming days as you pull together your marketing campaign.

The "Hot" Market Criteria

Once you know something about the demographic and psychographic characteristics of your target audience make sure they meet the following criteria:

1. They are easy to reach. You need to have an easy way to reach your target marketing once you create your product. You should be able to find your target market through the magazines they read, their professional affiliations and the websites they visit.

There are several different resources that you can use in order to find where your target market is hiding, but one of the best is the SRDS direct marketing list source. This reference features thousands of mailing lists and can give you a good concept of whether or not your market is easy to reach.

2. They have a passion for the topic. Golfers are fanatical about their sport. Shoppers love to shop. Parents of school-age children lose sleep worrying about tutors and coaches for their kids, or about whether they're saving enough for college. Your market should be just as passionate for their topic. Ask yourself if people are willing to give up money or freedom in order to be involved with your topic. If they are, they have passion.

3. They have money and are motivated to spend it. Just because someone is interested in a subject doesn't mean that person wants to spend money learning more about it. You need to make sure that your topic is "spend worthy". If there are magazines on the topic, chances are people spend money on it. Magazines are supported by advertising and if companies are able to spend money on advertising, they are selling products of their own to that same market. Check out Magazines.com for a comprehensive list of magazines in a variety of different markets.

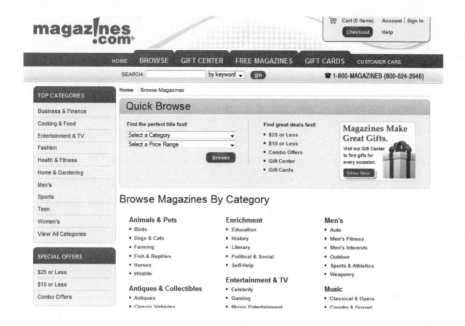

Magazines.com Category Page

By now, you might have an idea of the market you'd like to sell products to. But don't make the mistake of going too broad.

Let me explain.

You might want to sell your information products to "people who like to exercise". But, when you are selling online, especially an e-book, the narrower you can get your market, the better chances of your success. It's called "narrow casting" and it's very effective online.

Let's say you want to make a product for people who like to exercise. The only problem with that is that "people who like to exercise" is a very, very broad niche.

Here are some of the different potential sub-niche markets within the "exercise" category:

Age – Are you selling to teenagers, baby boomers, seniors, tweens, etc.?

Sex – is your product for males or females?

Goals – Are they exercising for weight loss, to improve in a sport or because their doctor told them to exercise to keep their diabetes in check? Maybe they want to compete in a bodybuilding or fitness contest.

Profession – Can you come up with exercise programs for accountants, attorneys, airline pilots, dentists, etc.?

Mode of Exercise – There are many modes of exercise that you could target your product to—runners, swimmers, power lifters, yoga, pilates, etc.

I think you get the idea.

The more specific you are with your target market, the better your chance at success. You want people who visit your website to think, "this is great, this e-book was written just for me!"

Another advantage of being laser-focused with your market is your pricing. In general, the more targeted you are with your market, the more money you can charge.

For example, maybe you can charge $20 for a general "small business marketing" product. BUT, if you turn that same information into a "marketing guide for accountants", a $50 or more price tag is not unreasonable because it is specifically targeted for that market.

The Occupations Rule

If you're still stumped for a market or a product idea, try out the "occupations rule". You will have the greatest chance of success when you sell your information products to "occupations".

I'm talking about jobs and careers like attorneys, firefighters, accountants, real estate agents, etc. Professions are easy to reach, they have a passion for the topic and they are willing to spend money on information that is specific to their profession. Selling products to professions meets all of the criteria for a "hot market."

The occupations are easily reachable – just about every profession has at least one national or international association. And many have local associations as well.

These associations have websites, newsletters, magazines and lots of meetings and events. It's quite simple to contact the associations and provide content to their members.

You can see a large list of occupations at:

http://en.wikipedia.org/wiki/List_of_occupations

Looking at that least it should be easy to come up with at least a half dozen ideas for a worthy market.

I've seen marketing advice that suggests it doesn't matter whom you sell to or what you sell, as long as you make your money legally and ethically. (And some don't even pretend to care about the law or ethics.) I disagree.

In my experience, you'll not only have a much greater chance for success when you choose a market and topic that interests you, but you'll also be happier and more satisfied with the work you've chosen.

Choosing the right market is absolutely critical to your success. Find the audience, serve the audience, and retain the audience—that's the foundation of your financial freedom.

Your Product

Now that you've figured out your target market, you have to determine how you will serve them. It's pretty simple: you will succeed with information products when you know your market well and solve a problem for that audience.

That's it! People like to make it a lot more complicated than it actually is.

All you have to do is figure out what problems your market has and then learn how to solve them. I've never done exhaustive research, or created complex 30-page business plans with graphs and charts. I just observe my target audience, identify their biggest problems, and solve them.

Maybe it's a frustrated parent whose five-year-old is still wetting the bed. Maybe it's a dedicated golfer who wants to know the inside scoop on the best local courses, or who does the best job custom-fitting clubs at the best price.

Here are some great resources to explore potential topics:

Ebay (http://listings.ebay.com)

Ebay is a goldmine for product and market research. The fine folks at Ebay spend a lot of time, money and effort testing which categories work best. Think about that – it's a billion dollar company has done all the research for you.

Don't try and re-invent the wheel.

Spend a few hours looking at the categories. And make sure to pay attention to the products being sold, selling price and the number of bids on these products.

Below is a screen shot of just a portion of the listings page at Ebay:

Antiques (297532)
Antiquities (6770)
Architectural & Garden (18595)
Asian Antiques (33370)
Books & Manuscripts (6884)
Decorative Arts (47603)
Ethnographic (7585)
Furniture (20365)
Home & Hearth (1405)
Linens & Textiles (Pre-1930) (12195)
Maps, Atlases & Globes (16160)
Maritime (3936)
Mercantile, Trades & Factories (1120)
Musical Instruments (Pre-1930) (453)
Periods & Styles (9020)
Primitives (17443)
Restoration & Care (138)
Rugs & Carpets (28092)
Science & Medicine (Pre-1930) (2677)
Sewing (Pre-1930) (3482)
Silver (49943)
Reproduction Antiques (2513)
Other (7783)
See all Antiques categories...

Art (344513)
Direct from the Artist (70725)
Art from Dealers & Resellers (266750)
Wholesale Lots (7038)
See all Art categories...

Computers & Networking (1801051)
Apple Desktops (2435)
Apple Laptops & Notebooks (4585)
PC Desktops (21353)
PC Laptops & Netbooks (40034)
Computer Components (332864)
Computer Accessories (572644)
Drives & Storage (141097)
Keyboards, Mice & Input (66429)
Monitors & Projectors (33896)
Networking & Communications (196220)
Printers (21488)
Printer Parts, Supplies & Accs (231419)
Scanners (4446)
Servers (14535)
Software (77710)
Technology Books & Resources (4368)
Vintage Computing (8463)
Web Domains & Services (8301)
Wholesale Lots (3306)
Other (15456)
See all Computers & Networking categories...

Crafts (738547)
Art Supplies (23498)
Beads & Jewelry Making (152408)
Glass & Mosaics (7954)
Handcrafted & Finished Pieces (12818)
Home Arts & Crafts (63919)
Kids' Crafts (5891)
Multi-Purpose Craft Supplies (23271)

Musical Instruments (353547)
Accordion & Concertina (1700)
Brass (6463)
Electronic Instruments (8701)
Equipment (8999)
Guitar (145413)
Harmonica (2919)
Instruction Books, CDs & Video (14013)
Percussion (28073)
Piano & Organ (4753)
Pro Audio Equipment (69810)
Sheet Music & Song Books (25515)
String (20356)
Woodwind (14936)
Wholesale Lots (306)
Other (1590)
See all Musical Instruments categories...

Pet Supplies (162216)
Aquarium & Fish (25732)
Bird Supplies (7889)
Cat Supplies (11364)
Dog Supplies (108917)
Horse Supplies (672)
Reptile Supplies (1812)
Small Animal Supplies (3330)
Wholesale Lots (951)
Other (1549)
See all Pet Supplies categories...

Pottery & Glass (340860)

You can search the completed listings in a specific category in order to see if there have been a lot of sales. Simply click on "Advanced search" and then enter your keyword terms. Click on "completed listings" to see how many bids have ended successfully.

You can see that the listings in green have been closed with a winning bid. If a majority of the bids have ended successfully, you know you've hit on a profitable topic.

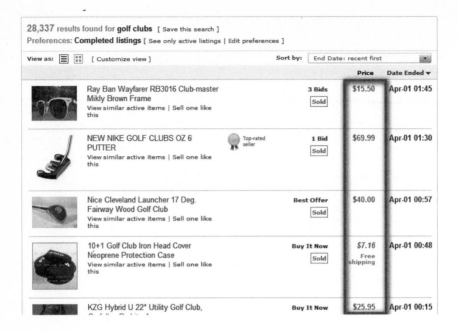

Ehow (www.ehow.com)

Ehow is a general information site that is populated with content that is created by a staff of freelancers and independent writers who have created content for the site. Ehow issues topic suggestions through their assignment system based on keyword and market research. Just like with Ebay, you can use the Ehow website in order to determine what topics are getting a lot of interest. If there are lots of articles on the same topic, you can be sure that a lot of people are looking for that particular topic. The great thing about Ehow is that each article includes step-by-step instructions, so not only can you get product ideas, but you can do the research at the same time.

How to **Get Your Baby to Sleep** Through the Night
How to **Get Your Baby to Sleep** Through the Night. Tired of waking two, three, four times every night to
http://www.ehow.com/how_11435_**baby-sleep**-through.html

How to **Get a Baby to Sleep**
Read, talk and sing to **your baby**. Even if she's too young to understand the words, the gentle rhythms ⟨
http://www.ehow.com/how_4254_**baby-sleep**.html

How to **Get Your Baby to Sleep** in His Own Room
How to **Get Your Baby to Sleep** in His Own Room. Many **babies** spend their first weeks or even month
bassinet, ...
http://www.ehow.com/how_2214162_**baby-sleep**-his-own-room.html

How to Make a **Baby Sleep** All Night
There are some well meaning experts who advise against this with the idea that **your baby** will become
...
http://www.ehow.com/how_4558383_make-**baby-sleep**-all-night.html

How to **get your baby to sleep** through the night
How to **get your baby to sleep** through the night. It can take a lot of patience to deal with a child who d
http://www.ehow.com/how_4465380_**baby-sleep**-through-night.html

(source: http://www.ehow.com/search.aspx?s=get+your+baby+to+sleep&Options=0&x=0&y=0)

MyGoals (www.mygoals.com)

MyGoals is a website where people can record their goals and share them with others. Products that help people reach their goals sell very well, so MyGoals can be a good resource for finding out what those goals are. Click through the different sections on the site to get ideas of what kind of goals other people are setting. MyGoals offers pre-made goal setting plans, like the one for traveling to Disney World below. You can look at the goal setting plans to see what type of information you may want to include in your product. By looking at the GoalPlans your research process will be even easier.

Set a New Goal: To Take a Trip to Disney World/Oı

This is one of our <u>pre-made Goalplans</u>, pre-loaded with common obstacles, tasks, and du

Browse our <u>directory</u> to adopt as many pre-made Goalplans as you'd like. Or use our <u>wiza</u>

Description:
Orlando is the world's most popular travel destination. Disney made the place a mecca in 1971, when it opened Walt Disney World, with the Magic Kingdom as its centerpiece. It was a big hit, synonymous with fantasy, fun, and family entertainment. Now Orlando is home to no fewer than 14 theme parks and many other attractions, and caters to the entire range of visitors, young and old, single and families. A trip to Orlando can be whatever you want it to be, but requires planning due to the wealth of options—and due to the large crowds. This Goalplan recommends that you start planning your trip at least two months in advance, and that you make travel reservations at least one month in advance.

Time to complete: Typically about two months

Adopt This Goalplan Now (You'll be able to <u>modify</u> it.)

Tell a Friend
about this Goalplan

Obstacle: I need to set a budget and save money.

Task: Set a budget for the trip	<u>Notes</u>
Task: Save money for your trip	<u>Notes</u>

(source: http://www.mygoals.com/pub-viewGP.jsp?goalPlanTemplateId=121&category=Appearance)

Discussion Forums and Online Groups

The Internet is founded on communication and it's clear that people go online in order to talk about their problems. Any popular topic will have a forum or a newsgroup that you can access in order to figure out what problems people are having.

Look through discussion forums to see what issues and questions come up over and over again. When the same questions are asked on multiple discussion boards, especially on multiple threads on a single discussion board, you know there's a problem in search of a product that will solve it. If you aren't already attuned to message-board culture, here are two places to start:

- http://groups.google.com
- http://groups.yahoo.com

Question Sites

Recently, a new type of site has become popular that is worth a look at for finding out what your market is interested in learning about. Question sites are sites that are specifically designed for people to ask questions on a variety of topics. You can browse through the question sites using your keywords to see what questions people are asking.

Look at these sites for questions and answers on your topics:

- http://www.answers.com
- http://answers.yahoo.com
- http://www.allexperts.com
- http://askville.amazon.com
- http://www.blurtit.com

Simply search for your keyword and a list of previously asked questions will pop up.

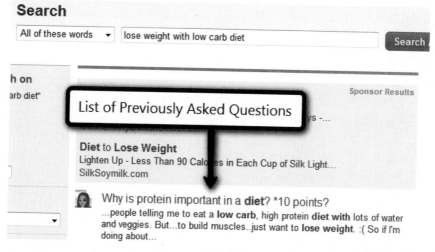

(source: http://answers.yahoo.com/search/search_result;_ylt=Aum4yEp3E5g8BVwY3tjfDsfj1KlX;_ylv= 3?p=lose+weight+with+low+carb+diet)

 **Today's Assignment:**

So now, on the first day, I'm asking you to make two crucial decisions:

-Who is your audience?
-What problem do they have that your product will solve?

Over the next 20 days, you'll learn how to create and market that product.

I can guess what you're thinking: What if I get to Day 7 of the coaching program and realize my Day 1 idea will never work?

First, I'd be surprised if the idea you settle on today doesn't have potential. But if you change your mind later, it's still not a problem. Choose something else and go through the process again from the beginning.

Day 2:
Map Out Your Online Empire!

Your Map Starts Today

On Day 1, you chose a target audience and a topic designed to solve a specific problem for the members of that audience. Now the real fun begins - You're going to map out the strategy for your online information-marketing empire!

Yes, you read that right. This book will have you begin with just one product (an e-book) but it's really the foundation of an empire. Through this process you'll begin to look at the big picture. The really big money comes after you made your first sale.

This is the part most people slip up. I've consulted with some experts who were really well known in their fields. If you plugged their names into Google, you'd get hundreds of thousands of search-engine hits. But they had no concept of the importance of this step.

They thought all they had to do was write a book, sit back, and watch the money roll in.

The ones who tried it before they came to me quickly learned that it doesn't work that way. Instead, you must **create a mix of products at different price points.** I made that bold and put that in italics so you wouldn't skip over it and miss its significance. No matter who you are, no matter how famous or brilliant you may be; you can never start with the assumption that it's easy to get rich with one book, or even to generate a modest but sustainable revenue stream. The bestselling authors in publishing history weren't obviously destined for that status.

Do you know how much J.K. Rowling got paid for her first Harry Potter book? Fifteen hundred pounds—a couple thousand bucks. And she only got that after the first 12 publishers had turned it down. John Grisham, an unknown lawyer in Mississippi, hand-sold copies of his first published book from the trunk of his car. He's worth a billion now, and he's doing all right. But they're prominent members of a very small minority: authors who get rich from a single product, or type of product. It doesn't matter if we're talking about fiction or nonfiction.

Just a handful of authors sell most of the books people buy. The rest of us need a strong backend program.

You've probably heard of the Rich Dad, Poor Dad series—hugely successful books, runaway bestsellers. The author, Robert Kiyosaki, started the series to help him market his more expensive backend products, including a financial board game that sells for more than $100.

I'll be blunt about this: I have the same strategy with this book you are now reading. You've probably noticed that I've mentioned ancillary products throughout the book. If you go to ryanlee.com, you'll see products and services that will help you continue to maximize your income as an online entrepreneur. You'll see a lot more of them as you go on in the book.

Does that mean Passion to Profits is part of some shell game, a scam? Hell no! It's a sincere effort to help you achieve financial success. It's a product that was designed for a specific audience—including you—with the goal of solving specific problems relating to building wealth online. And, yes, it's also part of a line of products. There's no contradiction between the impulse to serve an audience and solve its problems and having a well-thought-out sales strategy including backend products.

Your audience won't hate you for that. They'll thank you for giving them a choice of products at a variety of price points.

Let's get back to the things we addressed on Day 1: identifying your audience and identifying problems you can solve for that audience.

Do you think that any single product will address the entire audience? I don't. People have different learning styles. Some like to read, some like to listen to audio programs while others prefer live seminars and hands-on workshops.

Just think of the differences in the way people get to work. Someone who rides a bus or subway might prefer a traditional book. Someone with a long commute in a car might prefer to hear your message via an audio book. And you'll probably have customers who want to read while they're working, but can't open a book or listen to a CD while the boss is watching. But, she could get away with reading an e-book, which you'd sell as a downloadable PDF file. Many customers will purchase their first product from you at the lowest price point you offer. As they become more comfortable with you and your products, they'll gradually move up to more expensive products, programs, and services.

Don't Be Scared of High Prices

Early in my career, I was reluctant to create expensive products. But, then I discovered something interesting: The less people paid for my products, the less they valued them. I used to give free consultations. No one would take my advice. I raised my price to $250 an hour, and not only did I have more clients, the clients who paid that amount acted on my advice. I raised my price to $500 an hour, and saw the compliance of my clients double along with the price. Now I charge $1,000 an hour, and let me put it this way: I never have to repeat myself. My clients hear what I say. That kind of money has a way of focusing a client's attention. They hang on every word.

My friend Yanik Silver, a famous and extraordinarily successful Internet marketing specialist, knows the value of high-priced programs. His seminars and coaching programs cost as much as $15,000 per attendee. I can attest that there aren't many empty seats. The longer you're in this business, the more you'll understand that the higher the price you put on your products and services, the more value your clients will perceive. A percentage of your customers won't purchase a product unless it's expensive.

Product Categories for Empire Growth

Right now, I want you to do something simple:

Make a list of pricing categories for the audience you've identified, using the following chart. Then list the products you could create for that audience in each category. You can do this on your computer in a simple Word document, or with a marker on a whiteboard, or even with a pencil on a sheet of paper.

If you want to go high-tech, consider creating a mindmap, which lets you create a visual scheme of all your ideas. (You can find a great program at http://www.mindjet.com. And no, I don't have a stake in this one. I just like the products.)

Product Categories	Price	Examples	My Ideas
Introductory products	$5 - $50	Special reports, e-books, books, CDs, DVDs	
Mid-range products	$50 - $100	Software, multi-DVD sets, seminars, teleseminars, webinars	
Featured products	$100 - $500	Workshops, multiple-product kits	
High priced products *	$500+	Coaching programs, multi-day boot camps	

* Over time, the bulk of your sales should come from this category
I won't go into a lot of detail about these products for two reasons:
First, I could probably create an entire book about each one.

Second, most of you will start with an e-book as your introductory
product. As I noted earlier, e-books are ideal for getting your
business off the ground. There are no printing costs, and you
can fully automate the payment and delivery process so your
business is nearly completely hands off. Another benefit is that
you can update the content of your e-book quickly and easily. You
just have to make your changes and upload your file.

 **Today's Assignment:**

Today your assignment is to think about your marketing and do
one thing—map out all of the products you could create to serve
the needs of your target audience. Use a spreadsheet similar to the

one above and save it so you can refer to it later on. If you prefer, you can use a mindmap software program in order to branch out your ideas.

You should make sure to list at least one product for each price point in each category.

Day 3:
Beginning Branding – Choosing Your Domain Name and Product Name

Your Product Name

Now that you're on the road to creating your e-book you need to start thinking about your product name and your domain name. Your domain name is your calling card for your product and your product name is what people will search for.

You need to remember two things about product names:

1.They should be unique – You don't want there to be any confusion between your product and another product that is on the market.

2.They should be descriptive – You don't want your market to miss out on opportunity because they don't understand what your product is about.

Knowing these principles, here are some examples of some good titles and bad titles:

Bad Titles	Good Titles
ProfitMax System	*The Complete Guide to Profiting Online*
Hush-a-bye Baby	*7 Steps to Get Your Baby to Sleep*

Both examples have been improved by being more descriptive and more unique. "ProfitMax System" and "Hush-a-bye Baby" don't really tell you much about the products and there may be other products out there with similar names. The more descriptive and unique you can be – the better.

Try out a few title ideas but make sure to brainstorm at least a few as part of your work today.

Why should you decide on your product name before you begin writing your product? The title is going to provide focus for the rest of your outline and is going to help you figure out what you need to include in the product. For example, if you decide that the best title for your product is "The Six Week Guide to Having Your Baby Sleep Through the Night" you know exactly what you need to include in the product.

Finding the Right Domain Name

Once you've narrowed down a product title, you can begin to find the right domain name. Free domain names (like mysite.blogspot. com or freesite.wordpress.com) look cheap and if you look cheap, your market isn't going to buy from you.

Domain names cost about $10 to purchase for a year, and $10 to renew each year. It's the cheapest real estate you'll ever own, and potentially the most lucrative. There's no excuse not to get one! Millions of domains are registered each year, and most of the common words and names have already been claimed. You have three basic strategies for choosing one.

Descriptive
If your e-book is called "The Six-Week Guide to Having Your Baby Sleep Through the Night," you could use a domain name like babysleepguide.com or thesixweeksleepguide.com.

Titular

You can also choose a domain name that will mimic the title of the book. For example, for my product 4 Minute Diet the domain name is <u>4minutediet.com</u>.

Branded

A third choice is to pick a name that is either made up or has no real relationship to your products. The best-known examples are <u>google.com</u> (search engine), <u>amazon.com</u> (online retailer), and <u>monster.com</u> (job search).

I believe the best option is to create a combination of a title and branded word or phrase.

Passion to Profit is a phrase that I was able to easily brand as my own. But, if I called this book "The 21-Day Success Guide", and promoted it with <u>21daysuccessguide.com</u>, it wouldn't work. It's not a catchy or memorable title or domain name, and it's easily confused with other products and programs. Thus, it's a weak brand.

Look at your list of product titles and see how you can combine your product name and brand. Use the following steps to find the best domain name for your needs.

Seven Tips for Finding a Great Domain Name

1.Whenever possible, go with a *.com extension as your first option.Ifthedot-comversionofthedomainyou'veselectedistaken, don't automatically settle for *.net, *.biz, or the other alternatives.

Your customers will always expect you to have *.com. That's what they'll type first if they don't have a link to click through to your site. So if your first choice of *.com is taken, keep searching until you find one that isn't taken. This means that you might go through a half dozen domain ideas or more before you find the right one…keep trying! It will be worth it!

2. Make sure it's easy to spell. Take it for a test drive before you buy it. Say the domain name to friends and family, and ask them how they think it's spelled. If you've made a good choice, they'll get it right on the first try. This can save you a lot of problems later on down the road.

3. Avoid using words that have multiple spellings ("2," "to," "too," "two"). This is an invitation for imitators to copy your domain name and for your target market to lose out on your domain.

4. The shorter your domain name, the better. Try to make your title as short as possible while still making sense and fitting in with your branding efforts.

5. Avoid words that call to mind bigger brands and trademarked words. For example, eBay doesn't like to see companies use the word "bay" in their domain names. Legal challenges will sap your resources faster than you can profit off the name you've chosen.

6. Find a domain name that can be branded by you, which means avoiding generic names and phrases that can easily be copied. If you take the time now to find a good branded name it will serve you for years to come.

7. Brainstorm names at <u>thesaurus.com</u>. Sometimes you will be able to get a domain name of a slightly related word to your main word that you may not have thought of.

Invest in Domain Names – More Is Better

The title of your product and your domain name are inextricably linked. If the title of your e-book doesn't lend itself to a domain name that's still available, then you need to rethink the title until you come up with one that's a triple threat.

- It's a catchy title for your product
- It lends itself to an easily remembered domain name
- It's part of a brand that you can grow with multiple products at a variety of price ranges, as discussed on Day Two.

Once you settle on a domain name, buy all the similar names. That includes plurals and different spellings. For example, I purchased dozens of related domain names for one of my products called "Millionaire Workout".

- millionairesworkout.com
- millionaireworkouts.com
- millionairesworkouts.com

I don't think it's possible to buy too many variations. Get as many as your budget and imagination allow. Spend some time on the registration site in order to tap out your different resources. Register several domains at once so you can get complete coverage.

You can also buy domain names for future products. If you think of a phrase that would make a great title for an e-book down the road, get it now. I own hundreds of domain names. Some I use actively. Some I won't need for another year or so. Some I may never use. I see it this way: If you don't grab it today, someone else might get it tomorrow.

There are two other reasons for getting multiple variations on your domain name. The first is strategic: You can use multiple sites to test different promotions, incentives, and advertising tactics, and then track the sales.

The second is commercial: You can lend domain names to other people who're acting as your affiliates (you'll learn more about affiliate programs on Day 14 of the coaching program). I take the importance of domain names so seriously that I set up a low-cost registration service for my clients.

For domain registrations, visit http://ryanleeinternet.com.

Yes, I do make a profit off this service, and in that sense I understand that my advice to register multiple domain names is self-serving. But, I also make it easier for you to follow my advice, not to mention making it easier for me to follow my own advice. Just type in your keywords in the "start domain search" box and you'll be able to see what is available.

One more point about domain names!

Some of you may come up with a great title, but find that someone else owns it. Often, the owner isn't actually using the site, but instead owns it for the sole purpose of selling the domain at a profit. One company, http://www.afternic.com, sells domain names in auctions. Another, http://www.buydomains.com, sits on thousands of names that it sells to people like you for a premium price.

Should you buy an existing domain for more than it would cost to create and register your own? It's up to you. If you think you've found the perfect domain name, one that lends itself to a broad range of products within a single brand, it could work out for you. But more often than not, as a businessperson, you should launch your information products with as little up-front cost as possible. That includes getting a domain name for the minimum, $10 or less.

 **Today's Assignment:**

Today your assignment is to start brainstorming product names and domain names. You should write down at least 10 different product title ideas based on your product's purpose and your branding goals.

Then write down at least 10 different domain name ideas based on your product name and your branding goals. Write down plural versions and different spellings of your potential domain name idea.

Once you've settled on your product name and an idea of your domain name, go to http://www.ryanleeinternet.com (or a domain registrar of your own choice) and register as many different variations as your budget allows for.

Day 4:
Create a Product Outline

You've narrowed down your niche, you've settled on a product name and a domain name – and now it's time to write the darn thing!

You probably know someone who's working on the Great American Novel. Or the Great American Screenplay. Or some other grand project that he never comes close to completing. Chances are, you've started a book or two, and never finished.

Even if you understand that an information product isn't a novel or a major work of nonfiction, it can still seem daunting. That's a lot of blank space to fill. The best way to tackle any large task is to chunk it down into smaller, more manageable pieces. That's why I came up with this five-step system— it helps me follow a blueprint, allows me to use my time more efficiently, and makes the product-creation process more fun.

The Five-Step System

Your e-book won't be written overnight but it can be written if you follow this five-step system. Taking it step by step, you'll be able to get your product completed no matter how long your product is going to be.

Let's say you're going to write an e-book for new parents. You've done the research, and determined that the biggest problem new parents face is getting their baby to sleep through the night. Every part of their lives, from their health to their productivity at work, is affected by the baby's unpredictable sleep-wake cycles. That's the problem your e-book will solve by giving parents effective, real-world strategies, with the goal of getting their babies to sleep through the night in just six weeks.

Step 1: Select the points of interest

Choose 10 major points your book will address. This can be determined from the research you've done on the topic. For this topic your major points or topics might include "feedings", "naps", "nighttime rituals", "baths", "room environment", "music", and/or "massage".

Step 2: Expand upon your points of interest

If you just kept your e-book at just those 10 points, it would be a very short e-book and you couldn't charge more than $10 for it! You need to expand upon the topics with subtopics so that you have enough bulk to fill out your product and make it worthwhile for the buyer.

"Chunk down" each of these points into two or three subtopics that you can expand upon.

For example, the major topic of "Feedings" could be broken into three subtopics:

1. Morning feedings
2. Afternoon feedings
3. Evening feedings

Expanding upon these points gives you more to work with in terms of writing your product and can help you conquer the blank page without feeling so intimidated. Your research should be able to give you some information on what your subtopics should be.

Step 3: Write five pages for each subtopic

Writing five pages on one subtopic should be easy enough to manage if you've selected the right subtopics. With just five pages at a time, you'll be able to create a hefty product very easily.

Think about it this way – if each of 10 topics lends itself to three subtopics, and you write five pages on each subtopic, you have a 150-page e-book! If your subtopics don't easily lend themselves to five-page treatments, then go back and reconsider your choice of points and subtopics. Could some of the points be folded into another point? Are some of the subtopics so big that they belong on the original list of 10 points, giving them their own subtopics?

This is a great opportunity to hone your product before you've actually started writing it. This part of the process helps you organize the way you'll deliver those benefits.

Step 4: Start with your favorite subtopic

Let's stick with the example of the parenting book. If you love talking about your baby's bath routine, if that's your favorite part of each day, start there. The very first words you write will be about the bathing routine. It doesn't matter that the section on bathing doesn't come first in the book. Just start with them first in your writing process.

This helps you in three very big ways:

- First, of course, it's more fun for you, since you get to start with the part of the project that you're most excited about.
- Second, you get off to a fast start.
- Third, your enthusiasm and passion will set the tone for the rest of the book. When you go back to write the other parts of the e-book, that energy should come through to the reader.

Step 5: Hire an editor

I've made the mistake of skipping this step, and was embarrassed when I ended up with a product that had grammatical errors. So after your book is written, hire a good editor to check for logic, flow, grammar, and spelling.

That's it! Those are the five steps that you need in order to write a great product quickly and easily. It's the same five steps I used in order to create this product.

Beyond e-Books

You can use this chunking system of outlining and organizing for any type of product. Learning this five-step system will help you create more complex products in the future. With this same formula you can create:

- **DVDs:** Each major point can become a DVD chapter, and every subtopic should be two to three minutes long. Ten topics, each with three subtopics that take an average of two minutes to cover, will give you a 60-minute DVD.

- **Audio CDs:** This is very similar to the DVD idea. Each major point can be its own audio track. Or you can make each subtopic a separate track.

- **Seminars/workshops:** Extend this formula for a workshop that will last three days, or shorten it to create a one-hour presentation. If your subject material is rich enough, you might be able to build an entire seminar around each of your 10 major points.

 **Today's Assignment:**

It's time that your product started taking on a life of its own! Start your product creation process and write down 10 main points that you'll cover in your topic. Create subpoints for each of your main points so you have at least 30 areas to write about.

I'm giving you an aggressive assignment: starting with day 5, I want you to write five pages a day, covering an entire subtopic.

If you do that each day for the 17 remaining days of the coaching program, you'll have an 85-page e-book. I don't expect those 85 pages to be polished, or to represent a product that's complete and ready for sale, although you could very well accomplish that. I mostly want you to get the experience of working on a self-imposed deadline (and when you launch a business, almost all your deadlines will be self-imposed), while also showing you how easy it is to complete a project when you have a well-constructed plan. So get ready, you need to start tomorrow.

Finally, pick the subtopic you're most excited about and then begin writing tomorrow!

Day 5:
How to Create Your Products Fast

You learned on day four, some people take weeks or even months to write an e-book. But since this is a 21-day program, I want to give you some real insider secrets on how to create products quickly. How quickly? You can create a valuable, profitable product in less than one day—in a matter of hours, in some cases—if you use one or more of these nine shortcuts.

Speak it!

Sometimes we all feel as if we're bursting with ideas. We have so much information to offer that it seems to flow out of us like water, once we've opened the spigot. But there's the problem: To create a written document, that information has to flow through our fingertips to a keyboard.

Unless you're a professional writer, it's unlikely that your fingers can type as fast as your brain can generate ideas. But there are ways to get around that handicap. You can simply "speak" your product into a telephone, and a company called iDictate (idictate.com) can turn it into a typed manuscript. If you're really good at multitasking, you can dictate a book during your daily commute. The company charges between 1.5 and 2 cents per word.

Once you sign up for the service, you call the phone number, dictate your information, and let the iDictate typists transcribe what you say. They'll put the transcription into a Word document, and you either clean it up yourself, send it along to an editor, or do both—go over it once, then send it off. I love technology!

Among your other audio options, you can purchase a digital recorder and have those files transcribed by a freelancer. Or you can go really high-tech, and get a software program like Naturally Speaking (nuance.com), the basic version of which costs about $100. You speak into your computer microphone and let the program turn your spoken words into text.

Interview experts

Another way to create an information product quickly is to interview other experts. Experts add credence to your product and also make for quick product creation since you get your research done while you are creating the product.

For our baby sleeping product example, you can interview experts in the field. Each interview can be a separate chapter:

- A pediatrician discusses possible medical remedies.
- A dietitian explains how to manipulate the feeding schedule.
- A veteran nanny reveals tried-and-true methods for helping babies get into a consistent sleep pattern.

Other topics could include other moms sharing their sleep strategies. You can find mothers who've worked out sleep schedules in the most trying circumstances—with twins or triplets, for example, or when the family travels to different time zones or the parents work odd hours. If you want to explore something that's out on the fringes, you could talk to a Feng Shui specialist about how to arrange the baby's nursery for better harmony.

Think about your product topic and see if any experts would be a good match for your product. Write them a detailed email or make contact with them via a phone number asking for an interview. Make sure that they'll know that they get credit for the interview and have a link to their blog or site within your product.

Create a compilation

Another great type of information product is a directory, which is compiling and cataloging information that you have at your fingertips but would be difficult, if not impossible, for an enthusiast to find.

By definition these should be opinionated: "The 101 Best Underground Dance Clubs in the U.S.", for example, or "America's Top Family-Friendly Hotels". Start with the resources you know off the top of your head. If you run out of ideas before you have enough for your book, you can poll your extensive lists of contacts and resort to pure research and reporting. You can hire a freelance researcher to do some of this work for you. One company to help you with research tasks is TaskUs (www.taskus.com).

Hire a ghostwriter

This is one of the riskiest options. If you hire a competent and experienced ghostwriter, you could end up spending more money than you could to make off of the product. A less competent and experienced ghostwriter will give you a product that you may not want to put your name on. This is why I recommend hiring an editor and suggest handling the actual writing yourself. A capable editor can take your base ideas and turn them into a product for you.

You can find editors by searching on freelance bidding sites like http://www.elance.com or http://www.guru.com. We'll go over details of hiring through bidding sites in the sales copy section.

Purchase resell rights to an existing product

Many information marketers offer "resell" or "reprint" rights to their products, usually for a one-time fee. Expect to pay at least 10 times the retail price for resell rights, which allow you to make and sell as many copies as you'd like at the full retail price. This can be a winning proposition for both of you. The person who created the product has probably exhausted his sales opportunities, but if you have an audience he hasn't yet reached, you can make a substantial profit. Be sure to research the resell rights product thoroughly before you purchase it. There's nothing worse than buying a resell product only to find out that the market has been completely saturated with people who are selling the product for rock bottom prices.

Start your search for resell rights products at the following sources:

http://www.indigitalworks.com/
http://www.resellrightsprofessional.com/
http://www.website-affiliate.com/

Purchase Private Label Rights products

Another type of rights to look for is "private label" rights. These products, most often called PLR products, are completely yours to change and edit as you wish, once you make the purchase. You can find PLR products from a variety of different sources. The only catch is that the PLR product is sold to many different people at once. The same e-book, report or set of articles could be sold to 100 people or more.

If you're going to use PLR, look for limited license PLR where the package is only sold to a small group of people. As part of the purchase of PLR rights, you are also required to change the content in some way in order to sell it. For most infomarketers, this isn't a problem because even the best PLR products aren't written exactly to your specifications. You can go through the product and rewrite it on your own or you can hire an editor to make your requested changes. Either way, you can get a fully customized product in just a matter of a few days.

For PLR rights products, look to the following resources:

http://www.master-resale-rights.com/ (includes both resell rights and PLR rights products)
http://plrwholesaler.com/
http://www.theplrstore.com/

Record a live workshop

You can do a live seminar or workshop on just about any topic (auto repair, cooking, exercise). All you need is a place to hold the workshop and people to attend. Ideally, the participants will pay you to attend the workshop. But if you're just starting out, you don't even need that. You can get friends and family members to attend. Just make sure they look like people who're naturally interested in the subject on the recording. Record the entire event (you probably want to hire a professional video crew), put the footage onto a DVD, and you've created an information product in just one day!

You can also take the video and offer it as a "download" through your website. Now, it has a higher perceived value than just an "ebook".

I've done this with several of my seminars and boot camps, and found it works well all around. Not only is it profitable for me, but the videos are popular with those who wanted to attend but were unable to for any number of reasons.

Record a teleseminar

A teleseminar—a live conference call in which people listen in and/or ask questions—is a lot cheaper to produce and record than a live workshop. And when it's over, you can sell the audio as a CD or as a downloadable audio file. I charged $200 for my first teleseminar, which I held four years ago, and sold out all 100 spots, generating $20,000 in revenue. I've been selling a recording of the seminar as a CD set for $199 ever since.

There are dozens of services which provide large bridge lines for free. Here are a few resources:

www.freeconference.com
www.freeconferencecall.com

Record a webinar

Yet another hybrid product, a webinar is a combination of ideas 6 and 7—a live seminar or workshop you conduct through your computer. You can charge people to view the seminar, then sell the recording as a CD, DVD, or downloadable video file. You don't have to be a technical genius in order to record a webinar. You can use a service called GoToWebinar (available at http://www.gotowebinar.com) to automate the entire process for you.

 **Today's Assignment:**

Today is your first day of writing your first 5 pages. Before you get started, look over these nine methods of super fast product creation and decide if one of them is right for you. If you choose one of the methods, make arrangements to put your plan into action (ie: find people to interview, arrange for your webinar).

You can also use one of these methods to make just a single subtopic of your product easy to write. For example, if you can't find a PLR product that matches your entire product, you can find a short PLR report that relates to one subsection and repurpose it to fit within your longer product.

Day 6:
Make Your Product Irresistible

No matter how original, appealing, or well executed your product is; your sales will suffer if you don't create a good offer to your customers. A good product without an equally appealing offer means that you'll be leaving money on the table—sometimes a lot of money! Your goal is to create an offer so irresistible that your customers say to themselves, "I'd be crazy to say no".

People will make a purchase based on two calculations:

- How much value they expect to receive.
- The amount of risk they believe they're taking

They will measure these amounts against one another. If the amount of value they are going to receive outweighs the amount of risk that they are taking, then they'll make a purchase.

Today's lesson focuses on increasing the perceived value of your product so it will be easy for your market to make a decision to purchase your product. Since we're on a path to creating a product in 21 days, I'm going to skip the theories of consumer psychology and go straight to my favorite and most successful methods for increasing the value of your products in the eyes of your customers.

Packages and Combinations

If you were looking to purchase a product similar to the one you're offering your customers, which would be more appealing: a single e-book or a set of three e-books?

Packages are always more attractive – even if your package contains the same amount of information that the single product has. One of the best ways to increase the perceived value of a product is to break it up into components that can be sold as a set.

You can't do this if your product is an e- book that's only 100 pages long; splitting it into two 50-page e-books does nothing to improve its perceived value to your customers. But if your product is long and technically complex, your customer might prefer to receive it as a set, rather than as one potentially unwieldy volume. And you can sell two 100-page e-books, or two 60-minute videos, for more than you could charge for the same material in a single e-book or video.

Here's a real world example:

If you wanted to read J.R.R. Tolkien's Lord of the Rings, would you rather have a single book that's 1,200 pages long or three books that average 400 pages?

Even if Tolkien hadn't written the story as a trilogy, you would probably wish that he had. The most avid reader might hesitate before purchasing a 1,200-page book; buying three 400-page books, even at triple the cost of a single volume, is inherently more appealing and less intimidating.

I did this with my programs at speedexperts.com. Instead of offering a monstrous 600-page e-book, I sold it as 18 different programs bundled together for the price of one. One e-book would be tough to sell for $99, but when I offer 18 for $99, the offer becomes irresistible.

Finding products for your package

You can package complimentary products together and offer them at a lower price than they'd cost if sold separately. You don't have to use two of your own products; you can look for other authors in your field that might be interested in a one-time partnership. Look for authors in your field by doing a simple Google search or networking in a niche forum with other product creators. Many marketing forums have joint venture sections specifically made for people to connect with one another in this way. Make a post detailing what you're looking for and you'll be surprised by what you might find.

You can also search for products that are in the public domain— that is, not covered by copyright laws—and offer them as part of a package with your own creations.

You can also use any of the tips and ideas in the previous section to create products to add to your main product for a package deal.

No matter what method you choose to create a bundle, you should definitely consider making your standalone product into a bundle of products. The key is to raise the perceived value of your product or package of products without increasing the cost of producing or releasing the product.

How to use knockout bonus products that boost your sales dramatically

Another way to increase perceived value is to offer bonus products. Almost every company or individual that sells directly to consumers uses bonuses. I do it, and I recommend that you do as well. I'll typically offer at least one video, e-book, or downloadable audio interview.

Bonuses push the buyer from asking themselves "Should I buy this?" to telling themselves "I'd be crazy not to take in this incredible deal!" They are the icing on the cake and make your product offer completely irresistible. If you don't know what to offer as a bonus, here are some guidelines you need to follow.

A good bonus fits the following criteria:

- It must have a high perceived value to your customers, either because of the content or the format. Offering someone a downloadable audio or video, in addition to the product you want them to purchase, will always seem like a good deal. This is purely because an audio and video are seen as a higher perceived value than writtenproducts, even if they have the same exact content.

- The product must offer something that's either exclusive or, at minimum, hard to find. Nobody will be impressed with bonus products that can be found everywhere, or that everyone else in your niche is offering as a bonus.

- The total value of the bonuses you offer should at least double the price of your initial product. For example, if you're selling a $30 e-book, the bonuses should have a total value of at least $60. Your goal is to offer a bonus that presents a perfect complement to the original product. The bonus should be so appealing that your customers would be tempted to buy the product just to get their hands on the bonus offer.

For example, if your product is an e-book called "How to Make a Living Installing Home Theaters," a perfect bonus would be an exclusive directory of wholesalers that will sell home-theater equipment to contractors for 70 percent less than the retail price. Just one purchase from a wholesaler could be worth thousands of dollars in savings to your customer. Thus, you have the perfect bonus: The directory will have a high-perceived value, and mesh perfectly with the subject of your e-book.

That said, I want to throw out a word of caution: Don't go overboard with the claimed value of your bonuses. If you're selling a $30 e-book, don't try to convince your customers that the bonus CDs or audio downloads are worth $5,000. It sounds too good to be true, and your customers won't trust you.

Still not sure what to offer as a bonus? Here are a few more ideas to get you thinking.

- Do an audio interview with an expert or author, discussing a subject that touches on the subject of your e-book. For example, a baby sleep e-book could be packaged with an interview with an expert childcare provider.

- Give a directory of resources (wholesalers, experts, places to find consumers of a particular product) that will be valuable to your market. For example, an organic gardening video course could be packaged with a list of reputable organic seed banks.

- Share your personal Rolodex—all or most of your personal contacts in your industry (including names and emails)—which will help your customers jump-start their careers in your field. For example, a course on writing for the Internet could be packaged with a list of names and contact information for Internet copywriters and web writing teachers.

- Offer software that complements the product. For example, if you're selling a product on keyword research techniques, you can package a keyword research software that will help your customers find keywords quickly and easily.

- Give access to a private membership site that offers specialized information and access to people in your field. For example, a course on weight loss for those with celiac disease can include a forum where members can support one another and share recipes.

- Offer a free telephone consultation with you, usually 15 or 30 minutes (don't worry about an overwhelming time commitment; surprisingly, only a few customers will actually take you up on this offer.) For example, a graphic design course can include a session where you critique the work of the purchaser.

- Allow free access to a private teleseminar or webinar. If your product is on credit repair, you can hold a private teleseminar revealing a few bonus steps that aren't part of the original product.

- Share downloadable video clips that show step-by-step examples of how to use the information in your product. If you are selling a product on how to set up a blog to make money, you can offer downloadable video clips that will show the customer how to set up a blog from start to finish.

- Give e-books and downloadable reports that increase your customer's knowledge without duplicating information that's already in your product. This idea can apply to any topic because there is always something extra that can be learned. For example, a time management book could come bundled with tips for organizing or a DVD course on real estate investment could be packaged with a bonus product on property management.

Today's Assignment:

Figure out if you can offer your product as part of a package of products, or break your large product into several smaller products to create a package. If you can create a package and offer lots of value, go for it!

Brainstorm ideas for three different bonus products that you can offer with your main product. Think about the type of product you'd like to offer as a bonus and what would "make sense" with your main product. How does your bonus product add to the value of your offering?

You'll also need to create the next 5 pages of your product. Keep going…you can do it!

Day 7:
Sweeten the Deal with Risk Reducers

As I told you yesterday, people will make a purchase based on two calculations: how much value they expect to receive, weighed against the amount of risk they believe they're taking. Day 6 focused on increasing value to the customer. Now it's time to learn how to decrease a customer's risk—and in the process increase your sales.

Offer Powerful Guarantees

Imagine you're about to make a big purchase, like a flat screen television. You're nervous about making the purchase because it is going to cost a lot and you're not sure if you've made the right choice. There are so many choices out there when it comes to this kind of technology, and generally you're making a big investment when you buy this item. Electronics stores know this – and they utilize the "guarantee" technique in order to motivate people to make a purchase. Most offer a 30-day money back guarantee. This way you can buy with confidence and know that if you have a problem with your purchase you can get your money back.

Selling an information product has the same amount of risk. Although your product may be much less expensive than a flat screen television, there is added risk because they are purchasing from you online. They don't know who you are and they aren't sure if you are legit. The perceived risk for them is huge.

An information product requires the strongest and longest-lasting guarantee possible. In my experience, this guarantee translates directly to bigger sales and a longer life for your product.

You might be hesitant to offering a guarantee, for fear your customers will use the information in your product and demand their money back anyway. After selling hundreds of thousands of products online for over 10 years – I can tell you that yes, some will try and rip you off. But it's a very small percentage. Way less than 1%.

However, even with the occasional refund, you'll be increasing your overall sales by offering the guarantee. The increased sales generated by a strong guarantee will more than make up for the handful of customers who choose to abuse it. And here's one more thing to remember: In general, the longer the refund period you offer, the better your sales—and the fewer requests for refunds you'll receive.

Aim for at least a 60-day refund policy with no questions asked. Don't just promise something bland and vague like "money-back guarantee". Make it stronger and specific:

100% Money Back Guarantee!

We are so confident this product works. If your child is not sleeping through the night after six weeks, you can return this program and receive every penny back.

No questions asked!

Placing a box like this toward the bottom of your sales letter (which we'll get to in the next section) will offer your visitor powerful persuasion for purchasing your product.

The Keys to Terrific Testimonials

In addition to guarantees, you can also reduce risk by using testimonials. Going back to the flat screen T.V. example, if you have two friends tell you that XYZ brand is the best television based on their own experience, you're more likely to go for that brand. If you read Consumer Reports and it shows that XYZ brand is the best, you're also convinced that it's the right choice for you. You could also search Epinions.com for reviews from other owners to find out which television will be right for you.

You need to show potential clients that your product delivers the promised benefits. The best way to do that is with testimonials from happy clients.

Testimonials are the online equivalent of speaking with a friend. When it comes to information products, there aren't places like Consumer Reports or Epinions.com for your potential customers to visit. You have to bring the testimonials to them.

You may be thinking – "Wait! How am I supposed to get testimonials for a product that only exists in my mind and in my marketing plan?" You're not going to be able to get them yet.

What I want you to do here is list five potential sources of testimonials. Don't just list five friends or contacts. Throw a wider net. Who's the top expert in the area covered by your information product? Do you know this person? If not, how would you make contact with her?

Now, think of someone you know or have heard about who's had a disappointing or even disastrous experience in this area. How would you get this person to try your system?

Your goal here is to create a blueprint for acquiring testimonials that appeal to a variety of readers and evoke a range of emotions. Some people like to have an expert's opinion. Some want to know that other people in their specific circumstances have used this product, and that it was effective for them. Others are most concerned about safety. Remember, you set out to create a product that solves a problem.

Most infomarketers make a huge mistake when it comes to gathering testimonials. They ask their contacts in the niche or people they know from forums to read the product and give testimonials. While there's nothing wrong with this in theory, you need to have more purpose behind your testimonial getting. Testimonials are your best chance to show your customers that your product will solve their problem. They also give you the opportunity to show that the product passes muster with an expert, that it's safe, and that it's used by people who the customer can identify with on a personal level.

Match your testimonials to each major problem that your market may encounter when they are making their decision making process. If you can overcome their obstacles with your testimonials, they'll be more likely to buy.

Here's a list of types of testimonials to try and gather for your new product:

The expert testimonial – Find other experts who can vouch for your product. This is not the most powerful one, but it's still a good idea to have expert testimonials.

The average person testimonial – People don't want to undertake the problem solving process if it's going to be too hard. An average person can show them that anyone can make your solution work.

The newcomer testimonial – Having a newcomer testimonial will overcome your prospect's fear of not being able to solve the problem due to not having experience.

The tried and failed testimonial – Everyone, who has a problem with something in their life, has tried and failed to come up with a solution. If you can find a testimonial that allows your potential customer to see that someone just like them has tried to solve the problem and failed before finding your solution, you'll be able to overcome their resistance to buying.

Show Me the Proof

You now have two ways to reduce a customer's perceived risk: an ironclad money-back guarantee, and testimonials to the product's effectiveness and safety from a variety of sources. Now it's time for the final risk-reduction element:

Proof.

That's right: You need to show your customers **actual proof** that your program works.

There are several different ways you can offer proof to your customers on the sales page in order to show them that you're the real deal.

Case studies work best. Pick a handful of people or clients and have them use your product or go through your program. Record their results, and present them as case studies. Remember that there is a difference between your case studies and your testimonials. You aren't offering opinions about your product here like you would with testimonials; you're offering proof that the product delivers on its promise.

Sometimes that proof is easy to present.

- If you're offering a weight-loss program, you can show before-and-after photos, along with charts documenting changes in weight and girth.

- If you're teaching people how to make more money, you can show screen shots of bank and/or merchant accounts. Black out the actual account numbers, but show the changes in income, wealth, or whatever your product promises to increase.

- If your product is about shopping for discounts on fashion items and accessories, show a customer decked out in a killer ensemble, and show the price tags documenting the cost of these clothes vs. similar styles from top design houses that would cost many times more.

Based on these examples you can start coming up with some of your own case studies ideas that are appropriate for your market. Videos are always a great way to show off your case studies. Video may seem intimidating at first, but you can do about it in several different ways.

1. Traditional video cameras

You can shoot a traditional video with a digital video camera and upload it to your computer.

2. Record a web cam video

Skype offers free web cam calls, which can be recorded using additional plugins. Details are available at http://www.skype.com.

3. Screen capture videos

These are necessary if you want to show someone using your program in a video format. You can use a product called Camtasia, available at http://www.techsmith.com. The investment is well worth it when you consider how big of an impact this video may have on your conversions.

Payment Options

One final way to reduce risk is to offer a variety of ways to pay for your product. When people have options, they'll feel more comfortable with purchasing from you. How can you offer different payment options? It will depend on your product and your price point.

Here are a few examples of how you can give a variety of payment options:

Low monthly payments - These can be spread over a specific period of time, so a $200 product can be purchased in 10 $20 installments, rather than in a more intimidating lump sum. An initial investment of $20 doesn't seem like much at all compared to the $200 price tag.

Try before you buy - Customers can try your product for free before you begin to bill them. Depending on the product, you could offer a free one-week or even one-month trial before the first payment is due. This gives your target market a very low level of risk.

If it doesn't work, it's free - This is a risky, but potentially effective option. You're giving the product to customers and they're only obliged to pay you after they use your product and achieve results.

Name the price - Tell customers to pay you what they think the product is worth. This option puts even more risk on you, meaning less risk for your customers.

 **Today's Assignment:**

There are several different ways that you can reduce risk for your customers through your sales page and payment process. Deciding on these elements now before you start writing your sales copy (coming up in the next section) will help you focus your copywriting.

Decide what guarantee you will offer for your product. You should go with the largest guarantee that you can come up with. Go for a money back guarantee after a certain period of time.

Start coming up with the different types of testimonials that you'll use in order to prove your value to the marketplace. Brainstorm a list of people you can contact to show your product to once it's complete. You should have an expert testimonial, an average person testimonial, a newcomer testimonial and a "tried and failed" testimonial.

Come up with different ways to show proof of how your product works. Think about how you'll use case studies to reduce the risk for your buyers.

You're now up to page 15 of your product. Congratulations!

Day 8: Creating Your Sales Copy

You're now at a critical point in the process: Your instinct may be to rush ahead and complete your product all at once. I understand the urge, and applaud the enthusiasm, but I want you to hold yourself back.

Keep writing five pages at a time, but starting today you'll also need to start writing your sales copy. That's right....you'll be completing your sales copy before you create your product.

Your sales copy is designed to sell your product....but, you haven't yet finished the product. How does that work exactly? Isn't that putting the cart before the horse?

On the contrary, writing good sales copy can actually help you create a better product. Good sales copy describes the product's benefits. It describes the problem that it's going to solve for the customer. It tells the customer how it's going to make her life easier, simpler, more effective, or more fun.

When you write your copy first, you force yourself to think in terms of the customer: what the customer needs from you (the solution to a problem), as opposed to what you need from the customer (money).

When you do this right, and your sales copy becomes the blueprint for the best possible product you can create. I've written sales copy prior to finishing all my products, and my students work the same way. I can't tell you if it would work just as well the other way because

I've never tried it. So I confess I have no basis for comparison. I just know I get outstanding results when I write the sales letter first, and, like all my advice in Passion to Profit, I know it works.

Copywriting 101

Writing strong, persuasive sales copy is a skill. Like all skills, it takes time to master. I'd estimate it takes hundreds of hours of practice to get really good. But since this is an accelerated course, I'm going to give you the basics, pass along a few shortcuts I've learned over the years, and have you write a draft of a sales letter that will leave you with a sound template for your first product.

Your Headline

A strong headline draws the reader in, making it the most important component of your sales copy. If you can't come up with a good one, make the first two words "How to …". The rest of the headline should write itself. You'll almost never go wrong with a "how to" headline. Good headlines have a basic format. You can actually look at other headlines to get ideas for how to format your own. There is a huge list of headlines available as a "swipe file" here: http://www.directoryofezines.com/1fju56i8z/headlines.pdf. Use these headlines for inspiration but don't copy them exactly. You can also find some templates for creating winning headlines in this blog post http://www.copyblogger.com/headline-swipe-file/.

Create a hook

The hook is the part of the headline that will build interest and suck the reader into your letter. The headline is designed to grab attention and the hook will pull them in. It's often presented as part of the sub-headline or in the introduction of your sales letter. It should answer the questions:

- Why should anyone buy your product?
- How will it solve his problem?
- How is your product better than your competitors'?

Take a look at this headline and sub-headline combination from "Organic Gardening Magic".

**Start Saving *Hun
Organic Specialty**

**Soon you will easi
the organic food t**

Date: Wednesday, 7:26 AM
From: Laura Fox, Organic Gardener

(source: http://www.organicgardeningmagic.com)

The headline is in red, but pay attention to the sub-headline just below the headline. The black sub-headline answers the question that the viewers will have. The reader will want to buy the product because it saves them money and teaches them how to easily grow their own food.

Establish benefits

Many new copywriters make the mistake of focusing on the features of the product instead of the benefits. The features are the nuts and bolts of your product – for example, a 100-page e-book that instructs people how to get their baby to sleep. The features should be mentioned in your sales letter, but more importantly, you need to mention the benefits.

The benefits are the emotional weight behind the features. The book may teach parents to get their children to sleep faster…but what does that really mean for them? They will sleep better, feel more relaxed, be happier and their baby will be healthier.

List all of the benefits to your product. You can start by listing the features and then asking yourself, "Why is that important?" Keep asking yourself why until you hit upon the specific benefits that your market will get out of your product.

Use bullet points

Once you've created your benefits list you can look at them and decide which is the most important to your target market. Organize the benefits in a hierarchy—the ones that are most meaningful to the target customer come first—and give each benefit its own bullet point in your sales copy. Your bullet points should be written like mini-headlines. Look at the following example of benefits based bullet points from the Organic Gardening Magic Site.

Here's what you'll soon learn by reading "Organic Gardening Magic":

✓ **What Organic Gardening is and how to get started!**

✓ The Do's (and Don'ts!) of Making your Own Compost!

✓ **What you should never add to your compost or risk poisoning yourself and your family!**

✓ The Secrets of Crop Rotation and Companion Planting!

✓ **A Simple Yet Hardly Used Trick to Bring Your Fall Tomato Plants Indoors!**

✓ Why You Should Consider Raising Your Own Transplants

✓ **How To Build Healthy Soil (Even If You Are Working With Very Unhealthy Soil To Begin With)**

✓ Why soil pH is important, and how to correct it!

✓ **How to Recognize Your Friends and Your Enemies When It Comes To Insects!**

(source: http://www.organicgardeningmagic.com)

The major benefits in this list are linked to the knowledge that the customer will get from buying the product. This market is motivated by the need to get knowledge about organic gardening and their desire to make things easy.

Offer bonuses

We've already covered bonuses in detail in the previous section, but you'll need to create copy that plays up the benefits of bonus products. You should create a short list of benefits and bullet points for each bonus product.

Establish a need for immediate action

You have to create urgency with your sales letter so that the reader will want to take action NOW. Find a reason why people should buy your product today instead of putting it off. You can add extra bonuses that expire after a certain period of time. You can make your entire product a limited time offer. You can sell your product until a certain number of purchases or memberships are sold. You can also use external factors to add pressure (like taking advantage of a tax bonus that is about to expire).

The bottom line with your sales page is that you should **never be boring**. Every sentence has to sizzle and serve a purpose. If it isn't exciting, pump it up or take it out.

Shortcuts to Sales Copy Success

Looking over all of these points, you might be intimidated by all that you need to accomplish with your sales letter. The good news is that there are several short cuts that you can take in order to get the sales letter that you need.

Use a software program

As you've noticed, there's a formula for good sales copy. And where there's a formula, there's a software program to help you cut your writing time. Sales letter programs will allow you to put in your product information, your benefits and details into the program and the system will do the rest.

Try out the following websites for programs that I recommend:

http://www.saleslettergenerator.com
http://www.pushbuttonletter.com
http://hypnoticwritingwizard.com

Hire a copywriter

You can easily outsource the work. On the low end, you might pay $500 for a three-page sales letter from a solid professional. If you want the best in the business, expect to pay up to $20,000, plus royalties. If you've got a high end product, a professional copywriter is the only way to go.

If you decide you want to hire a freelance copywriter you can find one at the following sites:

http://www.guru.com
http://www.elance.com

Both of these sites are freelance bidding sites that will allow you to post your project request and have qualified professionals submit their bids. You choose the winning bidder and then the payment goes into an escrow account for safekeeping. Once the project is completed to your satisfaction, you'll release the money. The benefit of working with these sites is that you'll be able to evaluate the quality of the writers from their previous feedback. Your money will also be safe until you're happy so you'll be protected from a writer who will take your money and deliver low quality writing.

Learn to write like a pro

This isn't a shortcut; it's obviously the most time-intensive option since, as I've already noted, it takes hundreds of hours of practice to get really good at writing sales copy. I've been writing my own sales letters for almost 10 years and I'm still learning new and better strategies. But if you're serious about having a long, lucrative career creating and marketing information products, it might make the most sense for you.

It's often said copywriting is the world's most valuable skill. No outsider can ever understand the appeal of your products as well as you do, which means you're potentially the best author of your own sales copy.

Investing in your skills as a copywriter will pay off in the long run. There are dozens of products out there that promise to teach you how to create good copy. The best for entry-level writers, in my opinion, can be found at:

http://www.dankennedy.com
http://www.marketingrebel.com
http://www.moneyfingersinc.com

At this point in the coaching program, I want you to sketch out your own sales letter, in your own words. Even if you've decided to hire a copywriter or use a software program, I want you to hold off and try your hand at it first. The goal here isn't to write a perfect letter; it's to introduce you to the process of creating a successful letter. Your sales letter will inform the rest of your product creation process.

 **Today's Assignment:**

Even if you want to learn sales letter writing in the long term, you should work on your own sales letter now based on the resources that we've outlined in this section. Your assignment today is to write out a rough draft of your first letter and highlight the benefits of your product. Look into the options for taking shortcuts with sales letters like using software or hiring a writer.

Keep working on your five pages per day challenge!

Day 9:
Building a Website

Now that you've got the starts of your sales letter and your product is beginning to take shape, it's time to do something with that domain name that you purchased back on Day 3. You need to build a website to host your sales letter and your product delivery system.

Website Hosting

Before you can begin to design a website, you'll need a hosting package. Hosting can cost as little as $7 per month, so it's a small price to pay for having your own web presence. Your hosting company should provide you with space to host your website files, statistics monitoring and other basic features that will get you up and running. I highly recommend www.ryanlee.com/gator for hosting.

Once you purchase your hosting package, you need to get the Domain Name Server numbers from your hosting company in order to link the domain names you purchased with your hosting account. The DNS numbers normally look something like this:

123.domainhostingservers.com
123.domainhostingservers.com

Two numbers are required in order to connect your website correctly. Take these numbers and then go to your domain name registrar (for example, if you bought domain names from RyanLeeInternet.com you'd go to that site and login to your account). Select your domain and then select the option "Transfer Domain Name to Webhost" and insert the DNS numbers. Your domain will be connected with your hosting and you'll be ready to go.

Outsourcing Site Creation

If you can afford it, I recommend hiring a professional. You can get someone to design a nice-looking site with five to 10 pages for about $300.

There's no limit to the amount you can spend on website development, but I think there is a floor. Don't go for bottom of the basement prices! I once hired a college kid, and although I saved money, it was a nightmare to get him to update the site. It cost me in the long run.

You should always go with a designer who's a full-time pro. Check his references and online portfolio. Even someone who's recently launched his business should be able to direct you to sites he either designed or worked on. If he doesn't, steer clear.

Be as specific as you can when working with a designer. The more you streamline the process, the less it will cost, and the better the relationship you'll have with the designer. Write down exactly what you want for your site and you'll be able to communicate your needs clearly. The clearer your instructions are, the more likely you'll be able to get what you want from your outsourced designer.

Just like with copywriting, you can find freelance web designers at http://www.elance.com and http://www.guru.com. You can also find low-cost web designers at http://www.getafreelancer.com and http://www.rentacoder.com.

DIY Web Design

If you're so inclined, you can design your website yourself with a few simple programs. This isn't the easy way go about building a website for your product, but learning to develop websites is a smart way to build your business for the long term.

You can find hundreds of web-creation software programs, starting with Microsoft Front Page and Adobe Dreamweaver. There is also a free program called Kompozer. Each has a learning curve, and it might take you months to get good at any of these programs. You probably want to start with some kind of hands-on instruction—perhaps a continuing-education class at a local college—or at least an online course. Once you learn the basic principles that underlie all web design, it'll be easier to figure out which software program will work best for you.

You can also find Web-based template programs. (It shouldn't surprise you to learn that I have one of these at http://www.ryanleeinternet.com. Look under the "Build a Website" tab to get started.) These sites give you some basic templates to choose from, as well as an editing system to allow you to make changes to your site once you've logged on. Expect to pay anywhere from $5 to $20 per month for a template program.

There's no choice that works for everybody. A template program allows you to put up a site as fast as possible for as little money as possible. Learning to create your own sites takes more time, but gives you a skill that you'll be able to use throughout your career as an entrepreneur. If you get good at web design and find you enjoy it, you could save yourself many thousands of dollars over the years. The easiest choice, if you can afford it, is to hire a designer, with the goal of establishing a long-term working relationship that's mutually beneficial.

Steal This Website!

No matter which option you choose, you first need a really good idea of what you want the site to look like. No designer can read your mind, and if you expect him to, you'll spend a lot of money on revisions. Even if you're designing your own site, it helps to know what you want, rather than wasting hours staring at a blank page on your computer screen.

Short on inspiration? Make it easy on yourself: Find a site you like, and borrow your favorite design elements. Start with a simple Google search, using keywords that apply to your ideas for information products. Don't allow yourself to be inspired entirely by the first site you visit. Instead, spend some time clicking through a number of sites.

Take notes when you see something you like, paying close attention to these elements:

- Color
- Theme
- Layout
- Graphics
- Font (size and type)
- Navigation (top, left side, right side, etc.)
- How easy is it to get around the site

You probably won't find any single site where you like all these elements. But here's one of my favorite tips: If you find a site that you love, scroll to the bottom of the front page, and see who designed it. You'll often find a link to the designer's site. If it's not there, click through other parts of the site ("About Us," for example) to see if the designer is listed.

Corporate websites may not list the designer, especially if the company is big enough to have an in-house team in charge of its sites. But, if you're looking for ideas at corporate sites, you're probably wasting your time. Whatever you like about those sites could be out of your price range, or involve branding elements that you wouldn't be able to use. Save time and spare yourself frustration by studying sites that sell products like yours.

While you're looking at sites, keep in mind that your site doesn't need to have all of the bells and whistles that corporate and company sites have. Those sites serve different purposes. Your information product site should be focused on building your list and selling your product. Eventually, you may want to add a blog on the site, and additional pages to represent your other products as you expand your empire. For now, your focus is singular – look professional, be persuasive and sell your product.

At the very minimum, you need a sales page, an about page, a privacy policy and pages on the backend to deliver the product. Don't expand past much more than that to begin with. When you go hunting for examples of sites, make sure you're looking at sites that are designed for selling information products, and are not multi-page ecommerce sites. Those sites serve a different market.

Easy, Effective Design

You need to "keep it simple" in order to get through this challenge and get your site up and running. Don't bog yourself down with an overly complicated site.

A few rules to keep in mind:

- Keep your site basic, clean, and uncluttered. Your site should be serving one purpose – to sell your product. Keep all other elements that are designed for other purposes off of your page.
- Start off with a strong headline that offers a benefit. See the previous section for ideas on your headline options.
- Include an address and working phone number. Not only does this build trust with your customers, but it will help you avoid getting in trouble with the authorities.
- Make it easy to use your site. Use consistent, clearly labeled navigation links.
- Don't make customers work to find your links. They should be in blue text and underlined.
- The text should be easy to read: using white background and black letters is the only way to go.
- Keep fonts and sizes consistent. A large blue headline, followed by a small red paragraph, followed by black text with randomly placed blue words induces eyestrain. Your customers will leave before they even know what you have to offer.
- Don't use a Flash intro. Just take them to the text on your home page.
- Keep graphics small. The larger they are, the longer it takes to download your pages.
- Related point: If you decide to include advertising on your site, limit the number of flashing banners or animated graphics. They annoy customers and distract from your sales message.
- Keep the design consistent throughout the entire site. Your graphic elements are part of your brand. If your graphics are

jumbled and confusing, your customers will assume your products are messy and poorly conceived.

• Have a method to get each visitor's email address, which you'll use to follow up at a later time. This is the foundation for your online business! (More about this in a few sections).

Today's Assignment:

Today is a big day and your assignment might take a few hours to accomplish. You need to decide whether you want to hire a designer or go the DIY route. Once you've made that decision, decide what type of site you'd like to have and then start looking for examples of what you'd like to achieve with your site.

Evaluate five to ten sites in your niche to see what is common between those sites. Chances are if the other sites are using a certain color or layout, there's a good reason. Different markets of people respond to different site elements. If there is a common element between several different sites, you've hit on an important conversion element.

Once you know what you want, find a web designer using the sites listed above, start creating your own site or use a template program. Keep it simple – you can always make changes later. The important goal is to get something up so you can start driving traffic in a few days.

Don't forget to write your five pages for today!

Day 10:
Setting Up a Squeeze Page

Yesterday you built a website, but today it's time to build one specific page on your website that will increase your conversions, build your list and give you a place to drive targeted traffic. As pointed out in the last section, your product website should be focused and targeted on selling your product.

We discussed several important elements of your website:

- Your sales page
- Your privacy policy page
- Your about page
- Your delivery pages

These pages all create the backbone of a successful site, but there's one more page you need to consider creating for your sales website – the squeeze page.

A squeeze page is a page that is designed to get your visitor to sign up for your email list. It has a singular purpose. You're going to give away something for free in order to get your prospects to sign up for your list.

Let's take a birds eye view of what your website will look like with your squeeze page incorporated.

Visitors will arrive on your squeeze page and they'll take one of two actions – they'll either opt in to receive your bonus and join your list, or they'll leave the page. Those that opt into your list will be redirected to your sales page and see your main offer. That group will also take one of two actions – they will either make the purchase and then be redirected to the download area or they will leave your page. The beauty of using the squeeze page is that even if they leave the page after opting into your list, you can still market to them at a later date.

Building an email list is the foundation of building your online empire. If you create a squeeze page and take the time now to develop an email list, you'll reap the rewards for years to come. In the future when you create new products for the market, you can simply send an email out to your user list and you'll have instant sales. It all starts with creating your squeeze page.

Basic Elements of a Squeeze Page

Squeeze page design has its own set of rules because it has a singular purpose. The basic elements include:

- A headline
- A sub-headline
- A bonus description
- A benefits list for the bonus product
- A call to action
- An opt in form

Basically, you're creating a mini-sales letter for your bonus product. You won't go into as much detail as you will with your main product, but you do need to use the same basic format. Let's look at each of these areas in more detail.

Headline

We've covered headlines extensively in previous sections. Your squeeze page needs a compelling headline that will capture your traffic's attention and let them know why they need to read about your bonus offer.

Sub-headline

A sub-headline will explain more about what your bonus has to offer and what the visitor will get out of opting into your list and receiving your bonus.

Bonus Description

Your visitor won't want to opt in to your list and receive your bonus unless you tell them what it is. Try to use a graphic to represent the bonus product so there is more perceived value.

Benefits List for the Bonus Product

Besides being a free gift, what other benefits does your bonus offer? How will it help the visitor and what will they accomplish by opting in, downloading it and receiving it? Make a benefits list and develop bullet points based on those benefits.

A Call to Action

Your call to action will invite your visitor to opt in to receive the bonus. A simple statement like "Get Your Copy Now!" should be sufficient enough to motivate them to opt in – just be sure that statement is there!

An Opt In Form

Your opt in form will give your visitor a place to put in their name and email address so they can receive the product. Later in this section, you'll learn how an autoresponder program can help you set up an opt in form quickly and easily.

Additional Tips for Squeeze Page Design

Your squeeze page should be simple and to the point. The sales copy, picture of your product and opt in form should be the only things present on the page. You need to have links in your footer to your privacy policy and "about us" information in order to build trust with your audience.

Beyond that, you should keep things simple. Don't offer them links to other sections of your website, display advertising for other products or include additional articles on the page. Laser focus your squeeze page and you'll get better results. When you keep the focus on opting into your list, you make the decision easy for the visitor.

Here is an example from http://www.sahmwriter.com that illustrates the look of a clean and focused landing page.

Attention: If You Want To Make Money Writing At Home...

" Free Report Reveals How To Turn Your Writing Skills Into A Full-Time Income From Home Within Six Months Or Less...
Even If You Have NO Experience, NO Client List, and NO Portfolio!"

Get Your Free Report Now!
Just enter your information below
And you will be sent the FREE
"How to Make Money Writing"
report instantly!

Name

Email

Submit

(I promise NEVER to send you Junk or share your information, and I HATE spam mail!)

Access the free "How to Make Money Writing" report and you'll also discover:

- The <u>secret</u> to getting paid as a freelance writer, making $25, $50, even $100 an hour <u>or more</u> writing tiny one-page articles (no joke).

- A way to <u>get paid extra</u> for your basic writing skills, whether you work in an office, for yourself, or you simply want a side income.

- How to quickly have dozens of clients lined up, waiting for you to write for them, even if you've never written for money before.

- A site where you can find paid writing gigs every day - and we're not talking about making $2 an article. Get started today and get ready to put money in your pocket <u>right now</u> doing something you love (I'll share with you the URL).

- How to use *other* writers' mistakes to make yourself absolutely irresistible to your writing clients - with no extra work, just by being a person who values integrity.

- How to use the power of the internet to instantly find a LONG list of hungry prospects ready to hire you and pay you, <u>all completely legitimate</u> (you'll never need a 2nd job again).

- The quickest and easiest way to establish yourself as a polished, <u>professional writer</u>, and have prospects chasing you down.

- And much more!

Get Your Free Report Now!
Just enter your information below
And you will be sent the FREE
"How to Make Money Writing"
report instantly!

Name	
Email	

Submit

Even though it's split into two pieces in order for you to see the entire page, you can see all of the page elements at work. There is the headline, the opt in box, the benefits list and another opt in box at the bottom of the page. The visitor has no option other than to click away to another page or opt into the list.

Giveaway Bonus Ideas

Before you can build an opt in list or create your squeeze page, you need to figure out what to give away. Much like the bonuses that you'll package with your main product, your opt in bonus should be related to your product and help build value for the visitor. However, instead of being a supplement to the product, they should be a "lead in" to your main product and help motivate your visitor to buy your main product.

For example, for the baby sleep product, you could create a giveaway bonus product that reveals the "Top 7 Mistakes New Parents Make When Trying to Get Their Baby to Sleep." The product will be full of good information, but it will also highlight the problems parents are having with establishing good bedtime routines. At the end of reading the product, your list members will know what *not* to do, and in order to find out what they should do, they'll need to purchase the full product.

You can also highlight one important aspect of your solution in a giveaway bonus product. For example, if you have seven steps to getting a baby to sleep, you can include the first step in the bonus report as a "teaser" for your main product. The visitor will be informed by the new product, but they'll also be curious to find out what the rest of the process is.

Creating a teaser giveaway bonus will help motivate more users to take the next step with you and purchase your product. Just make sure that the bonus product has good quality information and is not just fluff piece that promotes your main product. Give your opt in list members quality along with your pre-sell.

Bonus products don't have to be very in depth. You can create a short report of 5 to 7 pages to give away to build your list. Simplicity is important because you really want your visitor to look to your main product for more information.

You can write your bonus product yourself and hire an editor to polish it for you, or you can use any of the methods discussed in the earlier sections for getting content. Once you create your bonus product, you can create a PDF of the document so you can easily distribute it. You can find free PDF creators at the following sources:

http://www.primopdf.com/index.aspx
http://www.cutepdf.com
http://www.pdf995.com

Using an Autoresponder Service to Build Your Opt In List

Once you've gotten your giveaway bonus product ready for distribution, you need to set up the framework to distribute it. You'll need an autoresponder service to collect email addresses and deliver your bonus product hands free. In the flowchart above, you can see that those that opt into your list will receive an email and a download link. This is how to set up that automatic email.

There are a variety of different autoresponder programs available for your use. I highly recommend www.ryanlee.com/aweber

For the purposes of this example, we'll be using screenshots from Aweber. Most autoresponder programs have the same basic options, so you should be able to adapt these instructions to your needs.

1.Upload your giveaway bonus to your hosting account.

You'll start by uploading your PDF to your hosting account. Your web host company should be able to assist you with this if you don't know how to do it. You can use an FTP program like Filezilla (http://filezilla-project.org/) to manage your uploads. After you upload your free product, be sure to note the URL where it is located. For example, if you upload your bonus product into a folder called "downloads" the URL would be:

http://www.yourdomainname.com/downloads/yourbonusproduct.pdf

This will be important to have later on in the process, so make note of it now.

2. Set up a new list with your autoresponder program.

After you've selected your autoresponder program and signed up for your account, create a new list. In Aweber, you simply click on "Manage Lists" and then click on "Create new list."

Manage Your Lists:

Unlimited Autoresponders   (+ Create a New List)
Click the list you wish to edit: Back Up & Export All Active Lists

Your autoresponder program will guide you through several steps in setting up your new list. You'll need to give your list a name. Your opt in subscribers will not be able to see this list name, so you can choose something appropriate for your records. On this page, you'll also need to add a list description, which your list members *will* see, so make the description appropriate for them.

As you can see from the following screenshot, autoresponder programs encourage you to use email addresses that come from your own domain and not a Gmail, AOL, Yahoo or any other free email addresses. You can easily set up an email address off of your domain name with your hosting account and use it for this purpose.

Essential Information

Enter some basic information about your list.

List Name: required

> bonusproduct900

✔ List name available!

List Description:

> Download free report on baby

"From" Name: Address: required

> Ryan

❗ Please enter a valid email address.

⚠ Avoid using free addresses like AOL.com and Yahoo.com.

Once you set up the contact information for your autoresponder list, you'll be directed to an area when you can set up the text of the email that your new subscribers will receive. Most quality autoresponders use a "double opt in" process which requires your visitor to confirm that they've requested the information you are sending them. This is an important feature which will reduce spam complaints and help your business be legitimate.

Part of the double opt in process is sending the new subscriber a confirmation email. Most autoresponders will allow you to customize this confirmation email. You should customize this email so that your subscribers will know what they'll be receiving. Imagine if someone opts into your list and then waits a day or two to confirm their subscription. They might completely forget what they opted into get and delete the email unless you tell them what they are receiving. Below, we've edited the confirmation email to reflect the title of the giveaway bonus product.

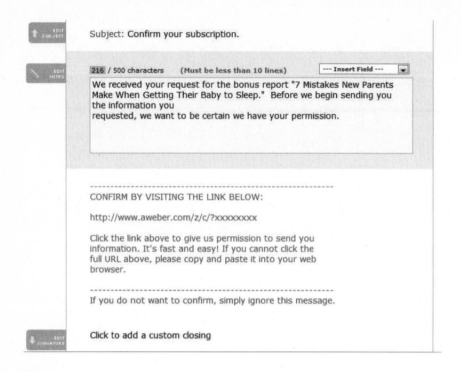

Subject: **Confirm your subscription.**

216 / 500 characters   (Must be less than 10 lines)   --- Insert Field ---

We received your request for the bonus report "7 Mistakes New Parents Make When Getting Their Baby to Sleep." Before we begin sending you the information you
requested, we want to be certain we have your permission.

CONFIRM BY VISITING THE LINK BELOW:

http://www.aweber.com/z/c/?xxxxxxxxx

Click the link above to give us permission to send you information. It's fast and easy! If you cannot click the full URL above, please copy and paste it into your web browser.

If you do not want to confirm, simply ignore this message.

Click to add a custom closing

The final step in getting your list set up will be establishing your "success page". This will be the page that your visitor will arrive on once they confirm their subscription. You can do this in two different ways.

•   You can create a download page that has a link to your free bonus report on the page.

•   You can link directly to the downloadable product.

If you go the second route, be sure to let the visitor know that they will be automatically redirected to the product in the confirmation email. Here's an example of placing the product download link directly into the autoresponder system so your visitor is automatically directed to the PDF.

Success Page What page of your website do you want to send people when they confirm?

Confirmation Success Page URL:

http://www.yourdomainname.com/downloads/yourbonusproduct.pdf

☐ Pass subscriber info (for personalizing this page.)

3. Create an opt in form so visitors can sign up for your list.

The final step in getting your autoresponder set up on your squeeze page is creating an opt in form, sometimes called a web form. A web form will give your audience members a place to put their contact information so that they can receive your bonus and become part of your list.

Most autoresponder programs will allow you to create a customized web form, and many offer several different design options. Here's the web form creation screen in Aweber. As you can see there are several different options for the look and feel of the web form (along the right hand top of the screenshot).

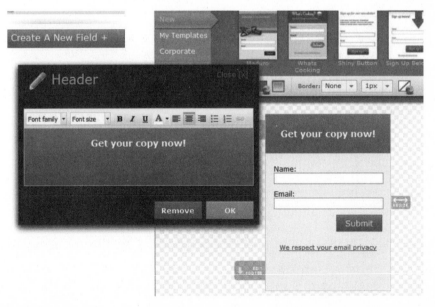

You can click on the header area and then add your own call to action above the opt in area. You can keep it simple, like the text above, or make a mini-headline to motivate the visitor to opt into your list.

In Aweber, the web form creation process is three steps. You choose your design, then you choose your settings and finally get the code to place within your website. The default settings can be used, or you can customize your thank you page and your "already subscribed page." Since we're on a 21-day challenge, just leave these settings as is and you can customize them later as you increase your branding efforts.

The final step is to get the code for your website. If you're building your website yourself you can copy the code directly and place it in. If you're working with a web designer, you can send them the code and have them add it to your website.

Your autoresponder program will generate the code for you and once you place it, your web form will show up automatically on your squeeze page. It will seamlessly take in names and addresses and deliver your bonus product without your interaction.

On day 12, we'll go over ways that you can use your autoresponder program to build trust and increased value with your list members. For now, focus on getting the automated giveaway product delivery set up.

 **Today's Assignment:**

Keep going with your 5 pages a day assignment and today add your squeeze page. Set up your squeeze page with the help of your web designer or on your own. Write a short bonus product, or have one written for you. Make sure that the bonus product pre-sells your main product. Get your product uploaded to your hosting.

Sign up for an autoresponder service and create your first list. Personalize your autoresponder set up so that your visitors know what they are opting in to receive. Customize your web form so it matches with your site's theme and copy the HTML code for safekeeping.

Write out your squeeze page sales copy and then place it on your site. Add your web form HTML code and then test out the form to make sure it's working. There's nothing worse than having your visitors reach a 404 error when they try to opt in to get free information from your site.

Now you'll have a squeeze page that you can start driving traffic to by using the techniques in later sections of this book.

Day 11:
Getting Paid - Credit Cards and Payment Processing

We've been talking a lot about selling your product and making money online, but how exactly do you accept payments online? Before we go any further in the product creation process, we need to get your payment acceptance process set up.

When I first started my online business, about half the payments came via checks in the mail. I had to manually enter all of the credit card numbers onto a printed form and call an 800 number to receive authorization. I was overwhelmed by the paperwork when my business started to take off, spending up to two hours a day just entering orders into the system.

Today, my business is on autopilot. I wake up in the morning and look at the overnight orders, and then go about my day without having to worry about hours' worth of paperwork. And it'll only improve from here: The technology keeps getting better, and the customers are more comfortable using their credit cards on the Internet. Still, you do have to make some choices before you can sit back and watch the orders roll in.

First, of course, you have to choose to accept credit-card orders in the first place. (Obvious, I know, but I do occasionally get questions from people who're sincere about starting an online business but wonder if there's some way around the credit-card issue. Trust me, there isn't.) Second, you have to decide if you want to get your own merchant account, or use a third-party solution.

Option #1 - Merchant account

With your own account, you accept payments through a financial institution of your choice, usually a bank. You pay the bank twice for each transaction. First, you pay a flat transaction fee, probably about 25 cents per order. Second, you pay a percentage of the sale price, usually about 2 percent. On a $100 order, the bank would get $2.25, and you'd get $97.75. Startup costs can range from $150 to $500 dollars, with a monthly minimum of $10 to $50 a month. By this, it means that the fees your sales generate must meet or exceed the monthly minimum set by your bank. If they don't, the bank will take out the balance from your sales revenue.

The benefit of having your own merchant account is that you maintain control of the payments. The downside is higher startup costs and more moving parts. You have to keep a close eye on payments, refunds, and chargebacks.

My merchant account is with a company called Power Pay (www.getpowerpay.com) I've been using them for over 6 years and I highly recommend them.

Option #2 - Third-party Merchant

These companies act as your merchant account. They process your customers' credit-card payments and send you what's left after they take out their percent. That percentage is a lot higher than you'd pay with your own merchant account, up to 8 percent of each sale. Although you give up more of your sales, there are serious advantages to starting out your business with a third-party vendor. The startup costs are low and the service is easy to use.

I've had good experiences with these three companies:

Clickbank (http://www.clickbank.com)

I recommend ClickBank as your best choice when you're ready to sell your first e-book. You pay a $49 setup fee, $1 per transaction, plus 7.5 percent of each sale. The biggest benefit of ClickBank is the built-in affiliate module, which allows other people (more than 100,000 are signed up) to sell your products. You choose the percentage of each sale that goes to your affiliates, and the company sorts it out from the point of transaction.

2CheckOut (http://www.2checkout.com)

This vendor has lower fees, but its affiliate option was still in the beta stage as I was finishing this book. You'll pay $49 to start up, 45 cents per transaction, and 5.5 percent of each sale.

Paypal (http://paypal.com)

No startup fee, but you pay $20 per month for the service. Fees are on a sliding scale, starting at 30 cents per transaction plus 2.9 percent of each sale. You can sell physical and digital goods.

Each of the three services I recommend allows recurring billing. This is a great feature when you create " --- of the Month" products or membership sites that require a monthly fee.

Tips for Smooth Online Processing

When you get approved for your own merchant account, it's important to maintain a good rating. If you're committing fraudulent or deceptive activities, the bank can shut you down and hold your money. Stay smart with your online business and your money will always be safe.

If you're going to do a big launch that will bring in large sums of money (that is, a lot more than your typical volume), give your financial institution a heads-up. I once forgot to tell my provider, and when I had a big surge in sales, they held up my money for several weeks.

To avoid chargebacks—which occur when your provider gets a complaint from a customer and credits his account, while taking money out of yours—make sure your customers know the name of the company that will appear on their credit-card statement. Tell them on the "thank you" page, which they'll see after a transaction is complete, and in your follow-up emails as well. For example, if your product is "The Complete Baby Sleep Solution" but your company name is "InfoProduct Publishers" make sure to state that the credit card transaction will appear under the former name instead of the latter.

 **Today's Assignment:**

Keep writing your five pages a day and look into the different payment processing options available. If you're starting out with information products, Clickbank is a good first choice.

Today is also a great day to catch up on any of the leftover tasks that you may have from previous daily assignments. Check in with your web designer, follow up with your editor and make sure all of your ducks are in a row.

Day 12:
Email Marketing Made Easy

The Money is In the List

What we've covered in the first eleven days is crucial to your success as an online entrepreneur. But if I had to pick one lesson that's more important than any of the others, it's the topic of today's coaching session. Your email list is the lifeblood of your business. This was hinted at in the squeeze page section, but now I want to make it absolutely clear.

It's more important than your product, your website, your logo, or the title of your e-book. It's the key to building wealth online. If you took away everything I have—my money, my websites, my products, my business relationships—and left me with just my email list and an Internet connection, I'd still be able to earn a full-time income. When you have a responsive list, you will always be able to earn money. How much money depends on a lot of factors, including some we've already covered: your offers, the perceived value of your products, and the perceived risk to your customers.

You might be surprised to know that the size of your list is less important than the relationship you develop with the people on your list. Let's say you have a newsletter that you send out regularly to the people on your list. A newsletter means one thing to you— it's a way for you to sell new products to your existing customers— but it means something else to the people who receive it. They expect a newsletter to include news. That is, information they can use. If you only try to sell, sell, sell, inundating your best customers with one pitch after another while offering them nothing of value, you will lose your customers. They'll unsubscribe to your newsletter and your orders will tank.

Once someone has opted into your list to receive your free product, you need to build your relationship with them. Even if they decided to purchase your main product, you should still be building a relationship with them in the long term. Email marketing allows you to become a trusted expert on the topic.

How to Build a Big, Responsive Email List

In addition to the squeeze page technique on day 10, you can use the following tips on the rest of your site to build a huge email list.

1. Make it easy to join. You want signup links throughout your site, easily visible, on every page. Use your autoresponder programs web form generator to place opt in forms frequently throughout your site. Think of the squeeze page example – there were two opt in boxes on that short page.

2. Sign up with online newsletter directories. These lists will not only put your newsletter in front of your target market but will also offer valuable backlinks to your website. Here's a short list of newsletter directories to get you started.

http://www.new-list.com
http://www.newsletteraccess.com/
http://www.listopt.com/

3. Gather email addresses offline. For example, if you're speaking at a seminar or conference, offer handouts or downloads of your slides in exchange for email addresses. If you have a booth at a trade show, give away T-shirts or water bottles in exchange for a business card. Double check the cards you receive to make sure that they have email addresses on them!

4. Look into co-registration services. These are programs that allow subscribers to join more than one email list at a time. Expect to pay fees ranging from 10 cents to a dollar per subscriber.

5. Team up with other newsletter publishers. You probably know people in your industry who have websites, sell products, and send out newsletters. (If you don't, you soon will; people who do what we do tend to find each other.) Some of these people will be direct competitors to you, but others will sell complementary products. For example, someone who sells exercise equipment isn't directly competing with someone like me, who specializes in information products.

You can team up with people like this by offering each other's newsletters. After someone joins your list, you can ask if they'd be interested in also receiving your associate's newsletter. Your associate would do the same. This doesn't work if you're selling competitive products. But if you're offering products that appeal to the same customers without directly competing with each other, this can be an effective way to build your email list as well as strategic alliances with your colleagues.

You can use the newsletter directories listed above in order to find complementary newsletters that you can team up with. For example, the baby sleep e-book newsletter could be perfectly complimented by a "make your own baby food" list or a "save money on baby purchases" list.

6. Create a "floating" box with a signup form. These features, which aren't disabled by pop-up blockers, ensure that visitors notice your signup form. Since I started them, they've increased response by up to 200 percent on some of my websites. The tradeoff is that visitors to your sites will consider them a nuisance, which is why it's doubly important to offer your customers something of value when they sign up. Your autoresponder service may be able to provide you with a floating opt in box option for your web form (www.ryanlee.com/aweber offers this) or you can hire a freelance web designer to find and install a code that will do the same. There are also third party programs that can generate a floating box for you, like Instant PopOver (http://www.instantpopover.com).

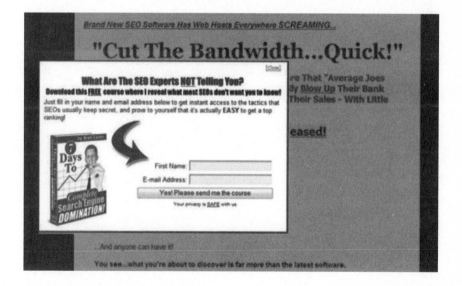

Email Newsletter Basics

How do you brand yourself with your market and build a relationship month in and month out? By creating a valuable newsletter. Having a valuable newsletter is the best way that I've found to make my mark in a crowded market, and having your own can be a good way to brand yourself and offer more value to your subscribers.

Many clients ask me if they should create their newsletter in HTML—a format that includes graphics and looks like a Web page—or stick with simple text. I've found that HTML newsletters work best for my list. However, you may find that the opposite is true with yours. You just have to experiment and see which brings you the best response.

Unsubscribe

You must offer readers a way to unsubscribe from your list. Most newsletter programs build this into your emails automatically. Don't take it personally when people unsubscribe. Every time you send out a newsletter, some people will unsubscribe, no matter how good your information is. This is a numbers game and you should focus on building the list more than worrying about how many people are unsubscribing.

Even though newsletters sent through autoresponders will normally include a clear unsubscribe link, you can also make your newsletter ultra-transparent by declaring at the beginning of the newsletter "You're receiving this newsletter because you agreed to receive the Baby Sleeps Well newsletter. If you no longer wish to receive this information, please click the link at the bottom this newsletter to be removed."

Frequency

More is often better. I've discovered that my newsletters are only effective if I send them out at least once a week. Even when I send five issues in a week, there's no noticeable increase in people who unsubscribe. But, as I was surprised to discover, there's usually an increase in sales. However, this only works if each issue has solid content.

You can pre-load your newsletter content and arrange it for specific delivery dates using your autoresponder program. You can create two to three newsletters ahead of time so that they are ready to go and you'll never miss a scheduled delivery.

Best days to mail

I've found that the middle of the week—Tuesday, Wednesday, Thursday—works best for me. But, just as with HTML vs. text, you have to test this with your audience. By pre-loading your newsletters and scheduling their delivery, you can be sure that you can deliver your newsletter on the best days for your audience.

Content

How you handle content in your newsletter is up to you. Your mix might include tips, interviews, answers to readers' questions, and some straightforward commentary. Just keep in mind that the goal of a newsletter is to get a response from your readers.

You can keep a schedule of what your newsletter will include so you can plan ahead for content. You should keep the content relatively consistent from issue to issue. This means that you should have an article, short tips list and interview each time, for example. Keeping the type of content consistent from issue to issue will serve several different purposes.

1. It will be easy to come up with topics when you know what you have to provide each week.
2. It will let your visitors know what to expect.
3. You can easily plan ahead – if you run across an article idea that will fit in tandem with an interview you have planned, you can save that article for your newsletter where the article will appear.

No matter what you decide to use as consistent content for your newsletter, you need to personalize your content. The worst thing a newsletter can be is boring. Nobody responds to vanilla. I believe that the personal touch is crucial. Subscribers to my newsletters know about my wife, my children, and my values. It's a great format for telling personal stories about yourself, as long as the stories you're telling relate to your customers and the products you're selling. Don't be afraid to get personal.

And you can't be afraid to speak your mind. As marketing guru Dan Kennedy says, "If you're not offending at least one person a day, you're not saying much."

Setting Up Your Email Newsletter Delivery System

In order to get your email newsletters up and running, you'll need to learn to use the broadcast message feature in your autoresponder program. Here's an example from Aweber:

Click on "create broadcast message" and then you'll be redirected to the message creation screen. The message creation screen for your autoresponder may be a little different, but you can get the basic idea from the Aweber window below.

As you can see from the screen below, there are several different areas that you'll have to contend with when creating your newsletter. The first area is the subject line. The subject line will get the audience's attention and convince them to open your email. Although your recipient has opted into your list, there's a good chance they might not recall who you are. Even if they do remember your name, there is a chance that they may have so many emails on a daily basis that they don't want to open the email unless they are absolutely motivated to.

There are two schools of thought regarding email newsletter subject lines. You can go the predictable route, and make sure that your email list members know that you are sending the newsletter that you promised. Sample newsletters subject lines could be "This Week's Herbal Medicine News" or "Accelerate Marketing Newsletter – Issue 957."

These subject lines are informative, but in my opinion, they are too boring to get good results. Imagine your inbox is full and you see one of the titles above. You like the newsletter and want to read it, but you don't feel like you have the time. Compare that to a subject line that says "Find Out the Top 5 Herbal Remedies That Could Save Your Life" or "The 3 Mistakes You're Making Right Now with Article Marketing."

Those subject lines are much more compelling and will motivate your audience to open up your email. You'll see an increase in your open rates if you use a compelling subject line that previews one of the articles in your newsletter.

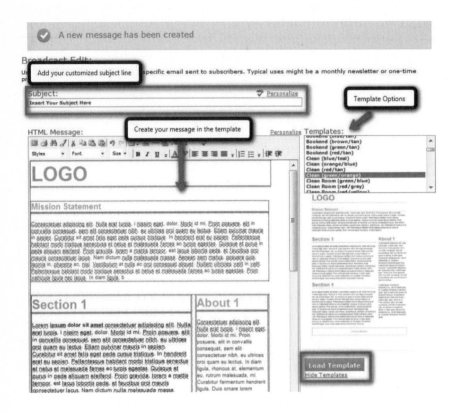

Other things to note on this page are the selection of templates. Your autoresponder program should give you a variety of templates to choose from your email newsletter. Once you select the template click "load template" and it will be ready for you to customize to your needs.

 Today's Assignment:

Add web forms throughout your site, in addition to the one that you have on your squeeze page. You should give your visitors several opportunities to opt into your list.

Brainstorm topics for your coming newsletters. Come up with enough content to fill at least four issues of your newsletter. Explore the newsletter creation options with your autoresponder program so you're comfortable using the templates.

Don't forget to write your five pages for today!

Day 13:
Affiliate Programs for Maximum Exposure

As you're beginning to develop your product, you're probably wondering how you're going to get the exposure you need in order to make sales with your product. We'll go over some important traffic building techniques, but for now I want to share the most powerful.

Imagine hundreds or even thousands of other people promoting and selling your products. Now imagine all of them doing this for free. All it costs you is a percentage of the sales price, which of course you only pay if there is an actual sale. It's not only possible; it's actually quite easy to do!

The concept is called affiliate marketing. (It's also known as associate marketing.) First popularized by Amazon.com back in the late 1990s, it's become a staple of online marketing. In fact, for about seven months of my life back in 2000, I helped run a large affiliate directory website. It was my first and only experience in corporate life, the only time I've been fired, and the only job I really hated. But as an independent businessman, I've used affiliate marketing extensively, and taught my students how to use it.

It's one of the best revenue-generating systems on the Internet. There are three ways to run an affiliate program. Two are relatively simple third-party systems, which I recommend. Your other choice is to install software and run your own customized program from your own website, which is too tricky to discuss here.

The Easy Choice

I'm going to make it easy for you.

For the purposes of your ebook, go with Clickbank (www.clickbank.com). The affiliate software is already built into the shopping cart. So there's no need to use a third-party service. That means you're ready to go!

How to Run a Successful Affiliate Program

Adding your product to the Clickbank marketplace isn't going to get hundreds of affiliates promoting your product automatically. There are several steps that you can take in order to make your affiliate program more effective.

Offer generous commissions

You want savvy affiliates pushing your products, and the best partners want to be paid well. Consider giving a commission of at least 50 percent of your sales. For most of my products and programs, I offer 50 percent. I go even higher on some programs. This is not a time to be cheap. Remember, it costs you nothing. Giving an affiliate 50 percent of a sale you wouldn't have gotten otherwise is a lot better than receiving 100 percent of nothing.

Clickbank allows you to offer up to 75% commission.

Put yourself in their situation: How hard would you work to get 15 percent of a $30 sale, especially if another potential partner is offering 50 percent commission on a similar $30 product?

The more money your affiliates can make, the more they will promote you. It really is that simple.

Make it easy to sign up

Your site should have links to your affiliate program on every page. A simple link titled "affiliate program" is just fine. Link it a separate page on your website that will offer more information about the affiliate program, including how much the affiliate will earn and how they can sign up for the program.

Provide tools

Create a resource page that includes samples of everything they'll need to sell your product— including text links, emails, classified ads, banner ads. Give a variety of graphics for them to choose from – you should have your graphic designer create several different sizes of your product picture. You can also create several different ad sizes. Your web designer can assist you with setting up simple copy/paste boxes that include the HTML code that your affiliates can copy and paste into their own promotion.

The following is an example of a fully functional affiliate page, located at www.bodybot.com/aff. In addition to the HTML copy sections, as seen below, the page also includes ads of many sizes and instructions on how to customize the affiliate links.

Free Affiliate Marketing Report: 3 Keys To Creating Big-Time
Commission Checks. Discover How To Increase Your Affiliate Sales
Month After Month By Downloading The Free REport At (Link To
Report Here)

In As Little As One Hour Per Week You Can Earn Big-Time Affiliate
Commission Checks By Promoting Other People's Products. Grab Your
FREE PDF Report To Learn How At (Link To Free Report Here)

Sample Solo Email to Promote the Free Report

[FIRSTNAME], 3 keys to getting big-time affiliate commission
checks

Hi [FIRSTNAME],

Have you ever been in the middle of one of those days when you
just thought, "It can't be this complicated! Can someone just
show me how to do it in a few easy steps?"

Some days it seems like a convoy of eighteen-wheeler trucks has
flattened me like a pancake on the "information superhighway".

ARTICLES

It's been proven time and time again that articles are one of the best way to sell products online.
WHY? Because unlike solo mailings, articles educate while they promote - *and these articles are no
exception!*

Where Can you Give Them Away?

Publish these articles in your

- Newsletter
- Ecourses
- Autoresponder

Build a relationship with affiliates

Email marketing lists aren't only for prospects and buying
customers. You can also build a list from affiliates to keep them
up to date on your product and offer them additional support as
it becomes available. Create a new list using the instructions in

the previous days and place an opt in box on your affiliate page. You can give away a free report on affiliate marketing (which you can easily find in PLR or a resell rights form) in order to encourage affiliates to sign up for your list. When you create new resources or launch a new product with an affiliate program, send your super affiliate list a broadcast message.

Offer powerful tracking and management

Experienced affiliates like to see detailed statistics, such as total hits and conversion rates. Using an all in one program will allow them to glean a large amount of information about their conversions, which they can use to track their results.

Take care of your affiliates

Answer their questions in a timely manner, and treat them as valued business partners. Staying in touch with an email marketing list for affiliates is a great way to be open to communication with your prized affiliates.

Pay on time

If you're using an automated system that pays your affiliates (like clickbank.com), you don't have to worry about making payments. Other software programs allow you to pay all your affiliates at once using paypal.com. Set a pay date and stick to it, each and every month.

Recruiting the Best Affiliates

The 80/20 Rule—also known as Pareto's Principle—suggests that you'll get 80 percent of your results from 20 percent of your efforts. Applied here, it's safe to assume that 80 percent of your sales will come from 20 percent of your affiliates. If you have 100 affiliates, odds are that 20 will drive most of your business, while the other 80 contribute little or nothing to your bottom line.

A handful of these "super affiliates" might come to you randomly. You have to recruit most of them. Here are three good ways to do that:

- Affiliate directories: Submit your program to some of the dozens of affiliate-program directories. This is the most scattershot approach, but may be your best choice when you're starting out. You can start out by submitting to www.associateprograms.com and www.affiliateprograms.com These sites will get you the most exposure, quickly, but is much less targeted than the two following methods.

- Manual recruitment: You can actively search for potential affiliates by searching keywords related to your topic. For example, if your product topic is singing lessons, you would search keywords like "voice lessons", "vocal coach", "how to sing", and "singing lessons". Visit those websites and ask if the owners would be interested in joining your affiliate program. Make sure to show them what is in it for them to promote your product.

- Convert current clients: Those who already use and enjoy your products could be your best salespeople. I already mentioned the importance of having links to your affiliate program on every page of your website. But your customers might see those links and not know they'd be good candidates, and that it's a potentially lucrative opportunity for both of you. So send out an email from time to time telling your customers that they can earn a commission for something they might already be doing—telling people about your products. Selling your affiliate program through your email newsletter is a great way to get people to promote your product who already have a positive experience with it.

You can't underestimate the importance of affiliate marketing, and its potential to build your sales volume exponentially. I recommend focusing 10 percent of the time you devote to your business on this area. Remember, it only takes a handful of productive affiliates and it can make your entire program successful!

 **Today's Assignment:**

Sign up for Clickbank.com so you can submit your product when you've completed it. In the meantime (after you write your 5 pages for today), set up your affiliate page with the resources that your affiliates will need to promote your product. Set up an affiliates list and create an opt in box on your affiliate page. Add a link from the other pages on your website to your affiliate page.

Once your product is up and running on your sales page, work on submitting your affiliate program to five affiliate directories. You should also find five potential affiliates by searching for related sites and contacting them about promoting your product.

Day 14:
Article Marketing Part 1 -
Writing and Submitting Articles

So far, I've had you do a lot of writing in these coaching sessions. You wrote a sales letter early on, and you've been working on an e-book. I had you create a newsletter and a bonus giveaway product. Now, continuing with that theme, I want you to start writing articles about the topic in your information products.

By "articles," I'm not talking about the type of journalism you see in the New York Times or Newsweek. The people who write and edit those articles are trained, experienced publishing professionals who belong to huge staffs of men and women with similar credentials.

You don't have to go to journalism school for the type of article I want you to write. Your goal is to establish your credibility in your market niche, and to drive traffic to your website by gaining wide exposure among people interested in your topic. In other words, you aren't trying to expose your work to an audience of millions, as you would in a mainstream publication. You want an audience of thousands, all of whom are intensely interested in your topic and could be persuaded to buy your products.

Unlike other forms of marketing, article marketing gives you a unique benefit of forming a relationship and proving your worth to your market before they even arrive at your landing page. When a member of your target market reads your article, they'll learn a little about your approach to the topic and how your product solves the problem. Articles can help you draw in readers and motivate them to visit your squeeze page. It will also provide valuable backlinks to your website that will build your search engine rankings.

I spend an hour or two a week writing new articles. I enjoy it, but more important, those articles help my business. These articles don't have to be 5,000-word essays. They can be as short as 300 to 500 words. Just make sure each one is informative, and try to find someone to edit it before you send it out.

Articles and Keywords

Your articles will have a much bigger impact if you build them around specific keywords that are related to your main topic. Keywords are terms that your market will use in order to look for information online. When someone comes online to find information about a problem they are having, they will type in search phrases into Google, Yahoo or whatever search engine they are using.

By using popular keyword search terms in your article, you'll increase your chances of being found by the right people. You can conduct some keyword research before you begin writing so you know what keyword terms to use in your articles. You should center each article around a keyword term. Use the term in your title, in your first sentence and two to three times in the body of your article.

There are several different sources for finding keywords, but one of the simplest to use is the Google Adwords Keyword Tool. The Google Adwords Keyword Tool is designed to help with Google's pay per click advertising program, but you can also use it for article marketing.

Visit the Google Adwords tool at https://adwords.google.com/select/KeywordToolExternal. Enter your main keyword phrase and then click on "Get Keyword Ideas" to generate a list of related keywords.

How would you like to generate keyword ideas?	Enter one keyword or phrase per line:
◉ Descriptive words or phrases (e.g. green tea)	baby sleep
○ Website content (e.g. www.example.com/product?id=74893)	☑ Use synonyms ▸ Filter my results [Get keyword ideas]

Choose columns to display: ⑦
Show/hide columns ▾

Keywords	Advertiser Competition ⑦	Local Search Volume: February ⑦	Global Monthly Search Volume ⑦	Match Type: ⑦ Broad ▾
Keywords related to term(s) entered - sorted by relevance ⑦				
newborn baby sleep	▭	3,600	5,400	Add ⌄
baby sleep schedule	▭	2,900	3,600	Add ⌄
babies sleep	▭	49,500	74,000	Add ⌄
baby sleep routine	▭	720	2,400	Add ⌄
baby sleep	▭	450,000	550,000	Add ⌄
baby won t sleep	▭	8,100	12,100	Add ⌄
baby sleep system	▭	720	1,900	Add ⌄
baby sleep training	▭	2,900	4,400	Add ⌄
baby sleep music	▭	6,600	9,900	Add ⌄
baby sleep problems	▭	1,900	5,400	Add ⌄
crying baby sleep	▭	4,400	6,600	Add ⌄

As you can see, there are various levels of searches for the related keywords in this list. Try to look for specific keyword phrases that have two to three words, like "baby sleep routine" rather than general terms like "parenting." The single word describes such a broad spectrum of information that you're sure to get lost in the competition, which includes major commercial enterprises. The specific phrase allows people who have a specific problem to find you. And you, of course, sell products that address the very problem these people have.

For the purposes of article marketing, you don't need to be too concerned with the number of searches, the number of competing results, etc, as you would with pay per click marketing or picking a domain name. Since you're going to be writing articles on a consistent basis, it's best just to select a long list of detailed keyword phrases that you can use at the foundation of your article topics.

Once you start placing articles on your website and distributing them to directories, you can look at your own traffic stats and determine where the most traffic is coming from. If you see that you are receiving a lot of traffic for an article on "baby sleep tips" you should create more articles around that topic in the future.

Article Ideas

The most difficult part of writing articles to promote your product is coming up with fresh topics. Although you've got keywords to work with, you can't just write an article on "baby sleep music". You have to come up with a compelling title and a fresh angle.

You can develop article ideas in one of two ways – you can either work with your keyword list and try to come up with an article title to fit those keywords, or you can come up with topics and retroactively insert your keywords into the title.

For example, you have the keyword "baby sleep tips" that can naturally be turned into an article "10 Baby Sleep Tips for New Parents." But you may also think of ideas that aren't keyword specific. You may read an article on herbal scents that help people relax and decide to adapt it for your baby sleep site. You can write the title "Herbal Scents for the Nursery" and then look over your list of keywords to fit an appropriate keyword into the title. Your new title and topic would be "Herbal Scents to Help Baby Sleep Problems".

You should get in the habit of keeping a list of potential topics for you to work with. Whenever you come up with an idea, write it down on your list. You may get ideas from reading the news, watching television, reading websites in your niche or just off the top of your head. Keep your list going and you'll never run out of articles to create for promotional purposes.

If you're stuck for ideas, try these six quick and easy suggestions, which come to you from Roger C. Parker's excellent book, Content Catalyst (http://designedtosellonline.com):

1. **Biggest mistakes:** What are the biggest mistakes your clients or competitors make? These articles can help pre-sell your audience on the natural solution offered in your product.

   Example: "The 10 Biggest Mistakes Made by New Chiropractors."

2. **Checklists:** These articles help show that you and your product are good sources for information.

   Example: "Ten Things to Do before Opening Your Own Shoe Store."

3. **Symptoms:** Symptoms articles help your audience identify their problems you're your product becomes the natural solution).

   Example: "Eight Signs Your Marriage is in Trouble."

4. **Resources:** Just like with checklists, resource articles help prove your worth to your target market.

   Example: "Ten Business Books Every Plumber Should Own."

5. **Trends:** Trends help you prove your value to the market and show how well you're keeping up with your industry.

   Example: "Seven Ways the Real Estate Crash Can Actually Help Your Business."

6. **Questions to ask:** Questions articles are informative and helpful.

   Example: "Five Questions to Ask Before Hiring a Babysitter."

How to Make Your Articles Work for You

Writing the article is only part of the process. The true benefit of article marketing comes from the bio box or resource box at the end of each article. You must include a resource box when you are distributing articles so your visitors will know where to go if they want more information. It will also create a backlink from the article directory where you distribute your articles to your squeeze page.

Your resource box tells readers how to get in touch with you for more information. If you give others permission to reprint your articles, make sure to tell them they must include your resource box at the end of the article. When you use a reputable article directory, the article directory will state a similar policy on their site.

Creating a great bio box the key to making article marketing work for you. There are four main components

A resource box should include five main components:

- Your name
- One or two sentences that describe your expertise
- Your keyword
- Your website's URL
- A call to action

Here's a sample resource box:

Jane Doe is a baby sleep expert who is dedicated to helping parents get more restful nights for themselves and their babies. For more on **baby sleep tips**, and to download your free report "7 Mistakes New Parents Make When They Are Getting Their Baby to Sleep", visit http://www.babysleeptips.com.

Note the specificity of that call to action, and how it entices the reader to click through to the website. In addition to the website URL being displayed in the bio box you should also hyper link your keyword to your website. In this example, "baby sleep tips" is linked back to the website. This will increase your site's ranking for that keyword. Most article directories will allow you to easily link your keyword to your site, but just in case, here's how you'd format the HTML:

```
<a href=http://www.babysleeptips.com>baby sleep tips</a>
```

Promoting Your Articles

Let's say you've written your article, had an editor take a look and offer suggestions to improve it, and written a resource box with an irresistible enticement to get readers to visit your site.

Now it's time to get the article out where people can see it!

Your website

This is the place to start. Place the articles on your site and create links to them from your home page. With a "directory" of articles on your website, you can increase your search engine rankings for the topics that you cover in your articles. Now search engines can find your articles and will direct people interested in your topic to your site. The more articles you have, the better your odds of being found by the customers you want. Don't forget to promote each article in your newsletter!

Article directories

There are hundreds of these online and their sole purpose is to list articles and provide backlinks. Many of these directories grant permission for other websites and newsletters to reprint the articles stored in their database, as long as the author's resource box is kept in tact. Each article directory will have its own specific sites.

There are a variety of popular directories that you can submit your articles to. Here is a short list:

http://www.ezinearticles.com
http://www.goarticles.com
http://www.articlesbase.com
http://www.articlebiz.com
http://www.articlesnatch.com
http://www.isnare.com
http://www.ideamarketers.com

http://www.article-buzz.com

http://www.amazines.com

http://www.articledashboard.com

In addition to these general directories, there are also many niche article directories that are set up to accept articles in a specific category, like law or health. Search for your keyword terms + article directory in Google to generate your own list of niche directories.

Before you add articles to the directories, you'll need to have some key pieces of information with you. You'll need your article title, a brief 2 to 3 sentence summary of the article, your article text and your keywords for your article.

You'll also need to select the category. If you aren't sure what category your article should fall under, do a search on the article directory using your keywords. Similar articles will show up and you'll be able to tell where your article should be categorized.

On the following page is an example of Ezine Article's submission page. As you can see, there is a category and subcategory to choose from. This will help classify your article and provide extra backlinking power. Your summary/abstract needs to be kept to 200 words max and then you'll be able to place your article body in the large box.

Ezine articles allows you to select a standard resource box that you can use again and again. Although this is a convenient option, it's not recommended that you do that. Each bio box should be customized to fit the keyword that you are working with. You can use the same basic template for each bio box, but be sure to change the keyword for better optimization.

Select A Category　　　　　　　　**Subcategory**

| Please Choose a Category ▾ | None ▾ |

Title Suggestions:

Select one of the titles from the box below to use it for this article.

Try a Title | Use a suggested title for your next article as a Platinum or Premium Member. Click here to learn more about Premium Membership.

Premium **Feature**

Article Title

[   ]

`100` Characters left

Abstract/Article Summary/Teaser Copy (2-5 sentences, no paragraphs please)

[   ]

Word Count: `0` (200 words max)

Next Autosave: `01:45`　No changes, nothing saved.Auto Save: On　**Turn OFF Auto Save**

Keywords (Comma Separate Please - keyword1,keyword2,keyword3,etc.)

[   ]

`100` Characters left

Author SIG - Resource Box

| Custom ▾ |

[   ]

Word Count: `0` (300 words max)

Each article directory will have a slightly different submission process, but the basics will be the same – use an optimized title, summary, keywords and proper resource box and article marketing will bring you a lot of traffic. Double check your spelling and submit your article. Within a few days it should be published and you'll start to see the backlinks and traffic come in.

 **Today's Assignment:**

Keep creating your book 5 pages at a time. Today, start doing keyword research to come up with a list of phrases you need to write about. Also begin your list of topic ideas. Use your keyword list as inspiration for your topic ideas or come up with ideas from your general knowledge or research and insert your keywords.

Write at least one article with a keyword, being sure to create a summary and a compelling resource box. Make a place for article publication on your website and post the article. Register for and submit to at least one article directory to start building traffic back to your squeeze page.

Day 15:
Article Marketing Part 2 -
Guest Posting and Submitting to Websites

In the last section, I discussed how to find keywords and topics for your articles. I also went over where to submit your articles – both on your own website and to selected article directories. However, there's another powerful publication opportunity that you can use to get more traffic (and potential buyers to your site!).

Publishing on established blogs and websites that are related to your topic will help introduce your product and your name to potential new customers. The beauty of posting to established sites is that they already have targeted traffic coming in. They are already serving your market and they have established credibility. By putting your content (and therefore your links and your product) in front of this audience, you have instant credibility.

Finding Related Sites

The first step in getting your articles on another site is finding a site that is related to your product's content. You can do a simple search for your keyword and find a variety of sites that have related content.

Publishing on someone else's site is often called "guest posting" so it's helpful to look for resources using that term. Guest posting on blogs is a popular strategy and a lot of blogs are in the practice of accepting guest posts. You can do a simple search on Google for your keyword + guest post which may deliver specific blogs or sites that are accepting guest post articles.

Guest posting opportunities are easy to find the Internet marketing and make money online niches. If your product fits into this category, you'll find the following list of resources helpful.

• 52 Blogs that accept guest posts - http://piggybankpie.com/guest-blogging/52-blogs-that-accept-guest-posts/

• 22 Blogs accepting guest posts - http://www.iwoodpecker.com/22-blogs-accepting-guest-posts-only-the-best-ones/

You can also connect with related site owners in forums and groups related to your topic. On Day 17, we'll look at forum marketing and how to connect with your audience where they are hanging out online. While you are marketing your product and offering helpful advice using the techniques in that section, you can also keep your eye out for related blogs and sites that users are promoting in their signature files.

For blogs, you can look at the directories Technorati (http://www.technorati.com) to find popular blogs that are in your category. The blogs in this directory are rated based on their popularity and frequency of posts. Here are the search results for "new babies" on Technorati. Make sure to click "blogs" when searching on the site, otherwise you'll just generate a list of posts that relate to your topic. While this might seem helpful, you'll really want to focus on resources that post consistently about your topic.

A final resource for niche products is to look to Sponsored Reviews (http://www.sponsoredreviews.com). Sponsored Reviews is a website that connects advertisers with bloggers who are willing to post reviews of products and services on their site in exchange for payment. However, you can use it as a research tool to uncover active and popular blogs in your niche that are open to some free content. You just sign up for a free Sponsored Reviews account and then search for your keyword term. You can filter the results by page rank in order to find the most established sites.

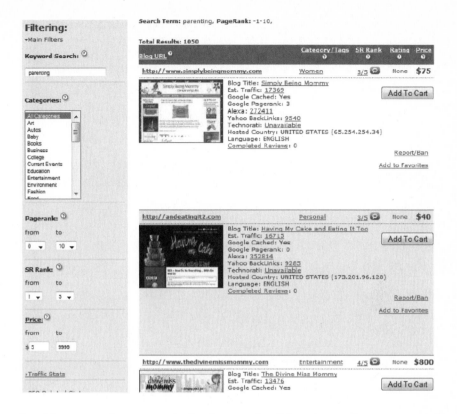

In this example a search for "parenting" has brought up several sites to choose from. At a glance you can see the popularity of the site, the existing traffic and a number of other factors. Keep in mind that not all blogs listed in Sponsored Reviews will be open to accepting blog posts. You need to figure that out independently, but it can be a good starting point for quickly and easily finding top notch blogs in your market.

Developing Your Pitch

Using the methods in the previous section, you should develop a list of potential sites and blogs where you want to submit an article. Before you start e-mailing them extolling the virtues of your article and asking for a mutually beneficial arrangement, you need to get to know these sites intimately. One of the biggest factors that causes a site owner to reject an article is that the article simply doesn't fit with the existing content on their website.

Review the blog or website and see what type of content is already there. Is there a particular slant or point of view that comes across through the articles? Are there ways of thinking or being that are criticized on the site? You want to align your article with the point of view of the site so that the owner will be more likely to accept your request to post there.

Spend some time investigating the site in question to get the feel of the site and discover what has recently been covered. When you contact the website owner, you want to have some ideas about what type of article you'll create. Offering a pitch for an article with your request will increase your chances of getting accepted.

Your pitch should be on a topic that is:

- Related to the host website.
- Related to your product.
- Genuinely helpful (ie: no sales pitches for your product)

If you've hit upon a great idea with developing your article topics, you can use one of those ideas for your guest post. Just be sure that you haven't already published the article. Your guest post article should be unique to the website where you're posting it.

Spend time on a blog commenting on articles if you're going to pitch a post there. Become part of the blog's community. This way when they receive your request to submit a post, it isn't coming from out of the blue.

Prepare your topics ahead of time so they can include them in your pitch, but don't write out the complete article. If you do, it can be difficult to find a place for that particular blog post.

When you contact the blog or website owner, keep it simple. Show that you know the website well and are confident that the topic will help the site's visitors. Keep it simple. Popular blogs may get tons of guest post requests each week and they are more likely to respond positively to a pitch that is short and to the point.

Here's a sample template you can use to pitch your blog posts.

Hi _____,

My name is _____ and my site is _____. I'm writing about offering a guest post for your blog/website. I have an idea for a post that I think your readers would really appreciate.

My intended topic is _____. (explain the title and a little about the content of the post). If that sounds like I good idea to you, I'll send over the post for consideration once it's done.

Thanks!

Creating Your Guest Article

Once you've gotten the green light from the website owner, go ahead and create your post. Keep in the mind the article tips that were covered in previous sections. Spend a little more time on your guest article than you would on an article that you are just sending out to the directories. A guest article is a showcase piece that will be your first exposure to that particular website's visitors.

You need to put your best foot forward.

Just like with article marketing, you'll need to use a resource box at the end of your guest article in order to direct the visitors back toward your website. You can use a resource box similar to the one that you use for article marketing but you may want to make it a bit more personal. You can share more details about yourself and connect with the website visitors.

 **Today's Assignment:**

Browse through the aforementioned resources to find a short list of websites and blogs that you can submit to. Familiarize yourself with those blogs and see what type of content that they have already posted. Brainstorm at least five different posts that you can submit to other sites and make plans for contacting them once your product is complete.

Don't forget to write your 5 pages for the day so you can get closer to completing your product.

Day 16:
Blog Commenting

Commenting on blogs can be an effective method of getting backlinks to your squeeze page and making yourself a known expert in your topic. Blog commenting is an ongoing strategy that can be used in the long term to generate buzz for your product. Make blog commenting a part of your promotion strategy, and don't forget to come back to this technique once you've finished your product.

Find Relevant Blogs

In the last section, I shared some techniques for finding relevant blogs in your niche. Although that technique was primarily aimed at finding blogs that post about your topic in general, with blog commenting you want to find specific blog posts that you can comment on.

Using the following techniques to zero in on blog posts that you can comment on:

1.Google Alerts (http://alerts.google.com)

Google alerts is a notification service that will send you messages when it finds blog content, articles, etc., which are related to a specific keyword phrase. Using Google Alerts can really save you time because you'll automatically be notified of new posts and you don't have to actively search for them.

You'll need a free Google account in order to use the service. Visit the Alerts website and you'll see the following screen where you can create your own alert settings.

Create a Google Alert

Enter the topic you wish to monitor.

Search terms:

Type: Blogs

How often: as-it-happens

Email length: up to 10 results

Deliver to: Feed

Create Alert

Google will not sell or share your email address.

There are a variety of options you can choose for your alert, but for blog commenting purposes, you should select "Blogs" for the type of alert. Enter your search terms – you can use more than one in your same alert – and then set your delivery preferences. You can have your alerts come straight to your inbox, but this can be really annoying throughout the day. Instead, you can set up your alerts to come directly to the Google Feed Reader.

2. Google Blog Search

While we're on the subject of the Google, you can use another Google tool in order to find more blog posts to comment on. Google Blog Search is located at http://blogsearch.google.com. Simply put your keyword terms into the search box, like you would with the regular Google search engine, and then look at the results. The search engine will generate results of blogs that deal with that topic and also specific posts that deal with that topic.

Google blogs `"infant sleep"`   [Search Blogs] [Search the Web]

| Blog results | Results 1 - 10 of about 10, |

Browse Top Stories

Published

Last hour
Last 12 hours
Last day
Past week
Past month
Anytime
Choose Dates

Related Blogs: Baby Sleep, **Infant Sleep**, Baby Sleep Through Night, Baby Sleeping - http://www.sleepinglikeababy.net/
Dreamtime Consulting: An **Infant Sleep** Consultant in Tucson, AZ. - http://dreamtimeconsulting.blogspot.com/
Sleep Solutions for Your Baby, Toddler, and Preschooler :: the blog - http://anndouglas.typepad.com/sleepsolutions/
Baby Sleeps Safe | Infant Safety Product - http://www.babysleepssafe.com/
Naturopathic Sleep Medicine Blog - http://drcatherinedarley.wordpress.com/

Children's Sleep Patterns – How Much Sleep Your Child Must Get ...
6 hours ago by Ottopedia
Sometimes it is recommended the **infant sleep** with the parents. However, if your infant experiences disturbed and restless nights it is best to have him or her sleep in their own be Sometimes placed in the care of a nanny or relative ...
Ottopedia - http://www.ottopedia.com/

Subscribe:

✉ Blogs Alerts
Atom | RSS

Parents learn safe **infant sleep** practices | Salisbury, NC ...
29 Mar 2010
Parents learn safe **infant sleep** practices. Bookmark and Share. Tuesday, March 30, 2010

3. Technorati search.

I mentioned Technorati in the last section as a way to find blogs for guest posts, and you can also use it to find specific blog posts. Make sure the posts option is selected when you use the search to locate posts that deal with your topics.

Making the Right Kind of Comments

Many info product creators try to use blog commenting as a backlink strategy, but they go about it in the wrong way. Blog owners are becoming more savvy and will likely delete comments that look too spammy or overly promotional. If you want to be seen as a trusted resource and not just another spammer, you have to make a quality comment.

Use the following tips to make sure your post is quality and not spam:

Read the post you're commenting on.

This seem like a no brainer, but you'll be surprised at how many people skip over this basic step. Just because the research tools tell you that a post is about "baby sleep tips" doesn't mean it actually is. You won't know what to comment about unless you read through the post.

Find something meaningful to say.

Posting "I agree!" is no way to brand yourself in your market. You need to formulate a quality response to the post. Add an additional tip related to the blog post or share a resource.

Keep your comment short.

Stick to one specific point for your comment and keep it short. If your comment is to the point, your comment will be more likely to be read.

Proofread and link carefully.

Before you hit "post" you need to double check the text of your post and your link. Blogs will allow you to place a link from your name to your website. In order to get the most out of blog commenting, be sure your link is written correctly and your comment is spelled right. You're trying to make a good impression with your comment, and bad spelling and grammar is no way to do that.

 **Today's Assignment:**

Even before your product is written, you can start commenting on blogs to get some backlink traffic coming toward your squeeze page. Today, your assignment is to set up your Google alerts for your keyword terms, and do some searching in Technorati and Google Blog search. Try to locate at least 10 posts that you can comment on.

Read through the posts and come up with some relevant responses. Make it a habit each day from here on out to find and comment on at least 5 posts per day. Don't forget to write your 5 pages from the day!

Day 17:
Forum Marketing -
Meeting Your Market Where They Are

Online forums can be a monumental waste of time, or a great way to drive traffic to your website without any money changing hands. I would've said "drive traffic to your website for free", but forums and message boards aren't really free—you're investing your time, and if you aren't careful you might invest too much of it.

Forums are simple enough to understand: They're online meeting rooms for people with particular interests. You register for free, and post messages as often as you like. Establishing yourself at a niche forum can provide you with a steady stream of targeted traffic, providing that you can find the right forum and make the right impression.

You can find forums for every interest imaginable, from aardvark grooming to zinc trading and everything in between. It's hard to think of a niche that's too small for an online discussion.

There are two main benefits for visiting and participating in online forums:

*   You'll learn a lot about your target market. You can tune in to what participants are talking about, particularly the questions they ask and the problems they want to solve. It's the perfect place to figure out what your next product will be. As you're promoting your current product, look for ideas for brand new products that you can create for the same market in the future.

- It's a great place to build your name. Message boards provide a terrific opportunity to establish your credibility as someone who wants to help members solve problems, and, more to the point, someone whose advice proves to be worthy of attention and respect.

Be careful with this last point. More often than not, this strategy backfires on people who go to forums with the sole purpose of selling products. If you get off on the wrong foot with the forum's leaders and regular posters, you'll be ignored, if not banned from posting again. That's why you need to follow my advice before making your first post.

At this stage of the program, more than two weeks in, you've visited dozens of websites related to your topic. Some of them probably have discussion forums. But, if you're looking for more, or for whatever reason haven't yet come across message boards specific to your topic, you can find them in seconds with a Google search.

Just type in "your topic + forum". For example, if your topic is horse breeding, you'd type in "horse breeding + forum".

Three more places to find targeted, high-quality forums:

- forums.google.com
- big-boards.com
- groups.yahoo.com

Before you decide to use a forum for research and for connecting with members, make sure it's active. Take a quick scan of the "most recent post" folder on the message board to see how often people are posting. If the last posts are more than a few weeks old, or older, skip over the forum. You won't be able to make enough impact.

Pregnancy & Childbirth				
Trying to Conceive Conception issues including, but not limited to, infertility	**heartburn? burping?** by amanda 04-03-10 07:42 AM		70	278
Pregnancy (1 Viewing) What to expect while you're expecting	**Fetal hiccups** by ferndoula Yesterday 01:10 AM		129	653
Childbirth From labor to delivery, topics dealing with the big day	**Scared!!** by ferndoula Yesterday 01:18 AM		55	325

Using Online Forums for Fun and Profit

Each forum has its own history, traditions, and levels of acceptable discourse. Most have moderators, one of whom is usually the person who owns the website hosting the forum. All have regulars, some of whom will gravitate toward each other and form cliques and in-groups. They might be nerds in the real world, but on this forum, they're the Internet equivalent of the football players and cheerleaders.

Nothing will get you banned faster than a dust-up with the moderators and most popular regulars. I've come up with four simple rules to follow when posting in any forum:

1. Lurk first

Before you make your first post, read through previous discussions and get a sense of the forum's personalities and protocols. Don't write serious, long-winded posts if the typical forum post is short and sarcastic. Conversely, if people are painfully earnest about the subject, don't jump in with funny retorts that could be construed as dismissive or offensive. The rules really aren't different from those of ordinary conversation, except you can't read the usual cues in vocal tone and body language. So the chances of creating the wrong first impression are very high if you're too pushy, careless, or disrespectful.

2. Always be helpful

Even if you're the smartest person on the forum and offer a product that will solve most of the posters' problems, you can't just come out and present yourself that way. The worst response you can offer is, "I'm an expert, and if you buy my book, your problem will be solved." Help people by offering honest, practical solutions, without asking for anything in return. Remember, it's a free forum. That doesn't mean the people posting on that forum won't spend money on a product targeted to their interests. But it does mean they're wary of sales pitches. Establish yourself as a reliable source of helpful advice, and forum regulars will eventually get curious about your site and the products you offer.

3. Create a strong "sig line"

Most message boards allow posters to create their own signatures—usually two to four lines of text under your name, which can include a link to your own website. Use this space strategically by offering something that's free to anyone who clicks through to your site. You'll actually be directing them toward your squeeze page, which will offer them your freebie.

Just as a reminder, here are some of the freebies you can offer on your squeeze page:

• Free e-book

- Free five-day e-course
- Free interview
- Free special report
- Free teleseminar

4. Don't get carried away

Sometimes you can get pulled into these forums and become a forum addict. If the regular posters sense that you need them at least as much as they need you, they'll be more inclined to see you as a buddy (if not a codependent) and less inclined to see you as an expert offering valuable advice. And it's surprisingly easy to get sucked into flame wars with other posters, which will destroy whatever credibility you've built.

You can't forget that you're the face and voice of your product line. You're the brand. If you're thin-skinned when people disagree with you or criticize your products (and if you have products, someone will find fault with them), or too quick to jump into heated, vitriolic arguments that have nothing to do with you, you'll alienate the very people you came to the forum to impress.

You can avoid getting hooked on posting, or getting too emotionally involved in other people's posts, by limiting your forum time. Set aside some time each week to visit your favorite or most promising message boards, and limit the time you allow yourself to read and answer messages. Set a timer if you need to. And whatever you do, don't allow yourself to get sucked into silly arguments and personal dramas. Remember, when you're online, you're working.

 **Today's Assignment:**

After you finish your 5 pages for today, find three good forums that are related to your target market. Lurk there for a few days to get the feel for each forum and then register if you feel like it will be worth your time. Set up your signature file to subtly promote your giveaway product.

Once you're comfortable with the flow of the forum, you can join the conversations. Avoid arguments, and be extremely cautious about promoting your products.

Day 18:
Online Video

When I first began publishing online, way back in 1998, online video was one of those ideas that sounded great in theory. Unfortunately, it just didn't work. There was no dominant, widely accepted format, and almost everyone had slow dial-up connections.

It could take hours to download a simple five-minute clip. Today, online video works, thanks to high-speed modems, more powerful servers and home computers, and the innovations of YouTube and many other sites. It's here, it's here to stay, and it's a medium that can benefit your business.

You can create video clips and put them on hundreds of free video-hosting sites for the world to see. Good video clips can quickly rack up thousands of views. If you have your URL on the video clip, it will drive boatloads of new visitors to your website, all of them looking for more.

There's another big benefit of these new video-sharing services. They host your video for free. Just plug some HTML code onto your site, and you have instant video. A final, and very powerful, benefit of online video is that it can allow you to rank highly for keywords that you just can't rank for otherwise. Google introduced integrated search in late 2009, which displays two to four video results as part of the regular search results.

How to Use Online Video Marketing

Your use of online video is only limited by your imagination. There are several different ways that you can use it. Here are just a few ideas:

- Create screencasts and publish them as a video tutorial. My favorite screencast program is Camtasia (http://www.techsmith.com). Camtasia will record everything that is happening on your screen and will help you create a professional quality video that you can upload and share. You can use screen capture video to record tutorials of software, processes or actions. You can also create a slideshow presentation and then take a screencast of your presentation.

- Edit clips from a live seminar and submit them to video directories. The seminar highlights will drive traffic to your website.

- Perform a webinar, record it, and spread it virally on the web. A great low-cost webinar program is Gotowebinar.com (http://www.gotowebinar.com).

- Create a short information video demonstrating your skill. For example, if you're selling an e-book on home remodeling, you can record a short demo of you installing a sink or putting up new blinds.

- Interview an expert, or be interviewed as an expert, and post that. Either interview can be conducted with a digital video camera, available at any electronics store. All you have to do is upload the video online, then post the link on your own site.

How to Create Powerful Video Clips

Most video sharing sites accept multiple formats. YouTube, the leader in online video, has this notice on its site: "YouTube accepts video files from most digital cameras, camcorders, and cell phones in the .WMV, .AVI, .MOV, and .MPG file formats." That gives you a lot of options, and removes just about any conceivable technical hurdles. That leaves this question: How do you create really good video clips?

Outsource when possible

Unless you're a video junkie, I'd hire someone to film and/or edit your videos. The learning curve for editing software can take a long time, so it's best to pay someone to do it for you. Look in your local Yellow Pages or online classifieds for wedding videographers in your area. They'll often work for a reasonable price during the week, when there aren't any weddings on the schedule. You can also search for editors on freelance sites like Scriptlance.com or Rentacoder.com.

Keep them short

While there are exceptions, it's usually best to keep your video clips under 10 minutes. Your customers don't want to spend that much time watching an online video, and YouTube and other online services don't accept clips longer than 10 minutes. If you need to have a long video, break it up into multiple clips that run five to seven minutes.

Get to the point quickly

Online readers in general have short attention spans, but with online video, you have even less time to hook your viewers. If you have one really powerful item to share, do it first. Don't wait until the end of the video, because they might not stick around.

Beware outdoor audio

Wind can wreak havoc on audio, as can cicadas, trucks on nearby roads, or just about any other type of noise. So before you make a big commitment to an outdoor shoot, test the sound and make sure you're going to end up with footage you can use online.

Don't get too fancy

In most cases, a $400 video camera is just fine for creating short, promotional clips.

Let there be light

No matter the price of the camera, what matters most are sound and lighting. Your customers have to be able to see and hear the information you're trying to convey.

Include your domain name throughout your video clips

Otherwise, people won't know how to find you. Editing programs can place a watermark on your video clips of your URL. You can also place the domain name in your screen capture videos.

Using these tips, you should be able to create a quality video to suit your needs. Now you just need to distribute it properly to get the backlinks and traffic you want.

Beyond YouTube:
How to Get the Most Benefit from Your Online Videos

YouTube, of course, is the number-one video-sharing site. As the property of Google, it will continue to grow. But there are other places where you can and should promote your video clips, including but by no means limited to the ones I list below.

http://video.google.com
http://www.revvr.com
http://video.yahoo.com
http://www.metacafe.com
http://www.viddler.com

You can register for all of these sites for free. When you do, select a user name that has to do with your URL, your business name or your product name. Try to get a user name that is close to your overall business name because you'll likely be using this same account to promote multiple products as your business grows.

As an additional way to connect your brand with your videos, make sure you register the .tv version of your domain name. If you already own yourname.com, you should also purchase yourname.tv. You can buy your .tv URL wherever you purchased your other domain names, as well as at my site, ryanleeinternet.com. Having a .tv name with further connect your product and business with delivering great video content.

Optimizing Your Videos

In order to get the traffic and the backlinks that you want from your video, you need to optimize your video. Keywords in your video won't appear in search engine results the way that keywords will be optimized in your written content. You have to go an extra step in order to optimize your videos.

When you upload your video, there will be specific guidelines for each video site, but most of them have the same basic options. Here is YouTube's video upload screen.

Name, Description and Privacy Settings

Title

Description

Tags

Category

Please select a category: ▾

Privacy

◉ Share your video with the world (Recommended)

◯ Private (Viewable by you and up to 25 people)

Save Changes

There are three different areas that you can use in order to optimize your video for your keywords. Use a keyword rich title for your video, much like you would with article submissions. The description area should be used to write compelling copy about your video that includes keywords and also a link back to your squeeze page. The tags for your video should be your keywords. Using these optimization steps will ensure that your video will get found by the right searchers.

 **Today's Assignment:**

Once you finish your five pages for the day, you should brainstorm some video ideas to promote your product. If you have a video camera, create a five-minute video demonstrating some aspect of your expertise, or showing how to do something related to your information product. You can also use screen capture software to create your video.

If your video turns out well, submit it to five video-sharing sites. Be sure to optimize your videos for your keywords and add a link to your squeeze page.

Day 19:
Viral Marketing

Viral marketing has an unfortunate name. The goal is to get other people—people who aren't working for you and don't personally profit from your work—to pass along your marketing message. The "pass along" part is how it came to be called "viral", although it's hard to argue that people pass diseases to each other with the same enthusiasm.

The first well-known example of viral marketing was Hotmail, the email service that launched in July 1996. When people signed up for free Hotmail accounts, the bottom of every email they sent would include a link back to hotmail.com, inviting the recipients to open free accounts of their own. Word spread quickly, and in just 17 months Hotmail had some 8.5 million subscribers! That got the attention of Microsoft, which snapped it up for $400 million. And that was in the dark ages of the Internet boom. A decade later, innovative marketers are using countless modalities and media to launch their own viral marketing campaigns.

My Smooth(ie) Experience

One of my earliest successes in viral marketing was an e-book called Smoothies for Athletes. It had 130 smoothie recipes (all of which tasted great, in my humble opinion), with complete nutritional information for each one.

I encouraged people to give copies of the e-book to family and friends. I also allowed resell rights. This gave anyone the ability to sell my e-book and keep all the profits. I knew other Internet marketers were looking for new products to sell to their customers, and a lot of them jumped at the chance for something they could sell at no cost to them. The savviest marketers packaged Smoothies for Athletes with their own products and services, using my e-book as a free bonus. You're probably wondering why I would give it away. It was, after all, a product that had real commercial value. On top of that, I'd worked hard on it, and was proud of what I created. This wasn't the marketing equivalent of a garage sale.

Here's why I did it: Throughout the e-book, I'd included links back to my websites. The more people who saw the e-book and clicked on the links, the more chances I had to generate business for my other products. Boy, did it work. And it keeps working. Today, four years later, there are tens of thousands of copies of Smoothies for Athletes floating around the Web, and they're still driving new traffic back to my sites.

Your Viral Campaigns

If I were going to try the same thing today, I'd use online video. In fact, I have used it, although not for my own business. I was touched by a three-minute video called "Free Hugs", which I saw on YouTube. I sent it out to my mailing list. (Do your own search and watch it. You'll see why I was moved.) The last time I checked, the video had already been viewed more than 15 million times. Of course, that's just one video, and there are millions of videos on YouTube alone.

Only a handful become truly viral and get seen by millions of people. But, you don't need millions to see yours. You might profit tremendously from a few hundred, or even a few dozen, if the people who see it are your target customers and send it along to other customers who need your products and services. I covered videos in more detail on Day 18, so I won't repeat all that information here, except to remind you of the top video-sharing sites:

http://video.google.com
http://www.revvr.com
http://video.yahoo.com
http://www.metacafe.com
http://www.viddler.com

Down 'n Dirty Viral Tips

Viral marketing can be powerful, but you need to keep the following tips in mind if you want to be truly successful with it.

Make it interesting

Boring reports and videos don't become viral. People only share it if it's exciting, thought provoking, and/or uniquely informative. You need to motivate them to take time out of their busy day to read your report or watch your video and pass it along to others.

Keep it short

Nobody's going to share a report or an e-book that's longer than 50 or 60 pages, or a video that runs past the five-minute mark. Shorter reports and videos are more likely to be passed along.

Keep your advertising subtle

You can include a short, promotional intro, along with a link back to your site. Or you use a watermark that includes your URL. (Someone sharing the clip might be able to edit out your intro or delete your link, but a watermark goes onto every frame of the video and can't be removed.) But, if your video is a pure advertisement, with no informational or entertainment value, it won't become viral unless it's so bad people send it around just to make fun of it. And that's far worse than getting no attention at all!

Help spread the virus

Put your video on your website, and give people tools to share it with others on sites such as <u>digg.com</u>, <u>furl.net</u>, <u>del.icio.us</u>, and others. You can link to your video across social networks, which is discussed in Day 22 and beyond.

 **Today's Assignment:**

Coming up with a viral marketing report or video is not something that can be done in a day, but today your goal is to at least start planning it out for distribution later on. By now, you've gotten to know your market intimately. You know what pushes their buttons, what gets them excited and what information will be likely to go viral.

Write your five pages for the day and then start developing an outline for your first viral marketing campaign.

Day 20:
Press Releases

Press releases have long been a staple in the world of journalism, but they've found new life as a tool for publicity and SEO. They can help you make an impact in your market and get you valuable backlinks. Before the Internet, press releases were designed to attract the attention of news editors who would place the news in their publications. Press releases today are accessible for everyone, including you!

Creating a Winning Press Release

An optimized press release can help you get exposure on sites that you could never reach otherwise. It will show up in the search engine results, like a regular web page, and will provide a backlink from the popular press release site back to your website which can make your site show up higher for your selected keywords.

There are three basic steps to creating a winning press release.

1. Figure out your newsworthy angle.

Press releases have to be newsworthy if you want them to be picked up by other website owners and accepted by press release distribution sites. Anyone can create a press release and distribute it, but you need to have a newsworthy angle. This means that your press release can't be purely promotional. You have to come up with content that has a fresh angle. If you're running a teleseminar, starting a new blog, releasing a viral product or launching your product – it's a good topic for a press release.

2. Use a catchy headline.

Your headline is the first thing that your reader will see and it's important that your headline incorporates your keyword as well as highlight a powerful part of your newsworthy angle. For example, a press release for your new product launch could have a headline like "Baby Sleep Expert Reveals Top Seven Mistakes That New Parents Make".

3. Incorporate your keywords.

The final part of creating a winning press release is to incorporate your keywords. The keywords should be used a few times in the first paragraph and throughout the body of your press release in order to be effective. Another big difference between old school press releases and new online press releases is that you can hyperlink keywords in your press release to your website. Most press release distribution sites set a limit of two links in the body of your press release. You can link the terms using the following HTML code.

<a href=http://www.yoursitename.com>your keyword</a>

Press Release Format

Unlike articles, which can be developed however you like, press releases have to follow a specific format in order to be accepted by press release distribution websites. Here's an example press release to show you the correct format.

(source: http://www.mediacollege.com/journalism/press-release/format.html)

Notice that the headline is added right after "FOR IMMEDIATE RELEASE". After the headline, you will need to add your city, state and the date for release. The first sentence is an expansion of the headline, and should include your keyword phrase at least twice.

In the body of the press release, stick to the facts and use an active voice. Pretend you're a reporter who is reporting on your launch or event and not the owner of the product. Add a few personal quotes about the importance of your product or how it meets the needs of the market.

The final section, after the main body of your article, is the summary. Some press release distribution sites will call this section the "about the author" section. It's very similar to the way that you use resource boxes in article marketing. You'll wrap up your press release with your address and contact information, including the URL of your website. You have to include your actual street address in order to comply with the press release site's standards.

Distributing Your Release

Once you have your release proofread and ready for distribution, you can choose from a variety of free press release services. Free and low-cost press release distribution sites only require registration and then you're able to submit your press release.

Here's a short list of press release distribution sites that you can use in order to get valuable backlinks and more traffic:

http://www.dbbusinessnews.com
http://www.seenation.com
http://www.pr-usa.net
http://www.openpr.com
http://www.free-press-release-center.info
http://www.i-newswire.com
http://www.prlog.org
http://www.przoom.com

 **Today's Assignment:**

Work on your press release to announce your new product. Follow the basic format and look to the many online resources available for developing a quality press release. Once your press release is ready to go, submit it to the previously mentioned press release distribution sites. Don't forget to write your five pages for the day!

Day 21:
Directories and Links -
Getting Listed Where People Search

Congratulations! You've made it to day 21! As you complete your last five pages today, you'll have 85 pages of content to work with. Now it's time to start building traffic and links to your site.

If you want to be successful online, you need to be in the search engines. That is, people have to be able to find you simply, quickly, and easily. There are only two ways to make that happen:

Natural search: Someone searches for you and finds you, or searches for your keywords and comes across your site. If you're on the Internet, you can be found this way, and of course it doesn't cost you a dime.

Paid listings: You pay to have your site featured for specific search terms. You only pay when someone clicks on your sponsored links. It gets a lot more complicated than this, of course. Lots of people have come up with lots of ways to game the major search engines, and get more visitors than you otherwise would have. You've probably deleted hundreds of pieces of spam promising to help you do this. Similarly, if you have an active website, you've probably gotten countless solicitations from companies that want you to buy paid listings.

We're not going to go over paid listings in this book for the purposes of simplicity. In the long run, it will pay off to have your promotional efforts focused on getting natural listings in the search engines.

A quick note about terminology: Search engines and directories are often grouped together, but they're different entities. Directories are categorized and tend to require human editing.

Two examples of popular directories:

• http://search.yahoo.com/dir
• http://www.dmoz.org

Search engines are automated. They employ "bots" or "spiders" to crawl through millions of websites, compile a list of links that contain your keywords, and then rank them according to their relevance to your search. The three most popular search engines are Google (http://www.google.com), Yahoo! Search (http://www.yahoo.com), and Bing (http://www.bing.com).

Keys to Getting Listed Without Paying

Search engines frequently change their algorithms to make it almost impossible for people to manipulate the system and get top listings. Companies like Google and Yahoo! hire brilliant mathematicians and computer scientists to ensure their search engines give their users honest results. There are, however, some basic ways to give your site the best chance to achieve a high ranking.

Submit to every search engine and directory - Every directory and search engine will have a place to submit your site for inclusion. The link might be easy to find ("Add Site", or something similar), but with some search engines you have to dig around. On Google, for example, you first click "About Google" then "Submit Your Content to Google".

Incoming links - The more high-quality links that point to your site, the better your search-engine ranking. For example, a link from the New York Times will hold more weight than a link from a small site with little traffic.

Articles - I've already discussed articles extensively in previous sections. Articles that are targeted for your keywords, submitted to directories and listed on your site will optimize your site for your keywords.

Create a blog - Search engines love blogs. Keep the content fresh, and you'll gain higher rankings with the search engines. *(Tip: Google now owns Blogger; you can bet that blogs using that platform will be noticed by Google's search engine.)*

Create videos - Submit them to video sites such as YouTube, which is also owned by Google. For more on videos, see the previous section on online videos and viral marketing.

Create a links page and ask for reciprocal links – In your research up until this point, you've discovered a lot of related websites in your niche. By creating a links page on your website, you can lay the foundation of a strong linking strategy. Contact these webmasters and offer to place a link on your links page in exchange for them listing a link on their page.

Age your page - If you plan on putting up a website in the future, put up a holding page right now. Then let it age. The longer it's been online, the higher your site will be ranked, even if there's no content initially.

My sites have great rankings because I stick with the basics I just described here: links, blogs, fresh content, and specific keywords.

Combine that with the rest of the strategies in this book, and you'll see your rankings rise.

Link Building 101

In addition to getting listed with the search engines using these methods, you'll also want to build backlinks, which are connected to your selected keywords. To put it simply, the more sites that are pointing at your site saying, "this site is about 'baby sleep tips'", the higher the chances are that your site will appear high in the rankings for 'baby sleep tips'.

There are several different methods for building links, as I've mentioned earlier in this book – creating and submitting articles, submitting videos, creating press releases, using forum marketing. All of these techniques, when used with your chosen keywords, will optimize your website for those keywords and build rankings in search engine results for those keywords.

Advanced Link Building

In addition to these techniques, you can also use two other techniques to build powerful backlinks and increase your rankings.

You have two choices:

First, you can build a links page, which is relatively easy and quick. However, if that's all you do, it pulls people away from your sales letter and sends them elsewhere. Once they leave, it's unlikely they'll come back and buy your product.

The second option is to create a separate website with nothing but content. This is where people will get to know you. They'll read your blog, see your articles, find links to your video clips, and get a chance to sign up for your newsletter, which means they become part of your mailing list.

But the biggest role of this site, of course, is to get people interested in your information products. The links to those sites will be prominently placed on your content site. Once you have a content site, you've given people a reason to give you reciprocal links on their sites. That is, they're comfortable with the idea of sending visitors from their site to yours. The more reciprocal links you have, the more new leads you can generate for your information products.

Creating a separate site is a lot of work, but also has some big benefits:

- Free traffic: You'll get visitors from places you couldn't reach with your own marketing. The better your content site, the more links you'll get. The best websites get thousands of links. If you end up with dozens of incoming links, consider your content site successful.

- Staying power: Owners of websites rarely take down links once they've gone to the trouble of adding them. I still have links to my sites from people who put them up seven years ago. The longer you keep your content site up and running, the more incoming links you'll have.

- Search-engine rankings: Search engines tend to give higher rankings to sites with higher-quality links. You're important to the search engines if other people think you're important enough to link to you.

How to Get More Links

The most common way to start a link campaign is to do a Google search of your targeted, find complementary but non-competitive websites, and ask for reciprocal links. Make the appeal to the site's owner personal—if it reads like a form letter, she'll delete it without considering your offer. If you're asking a stranger for a reciprocal link, you first need to show that you've already done your part. So make sure you show her exactly where the link to her site is.

If the site you're targeting has multiple sets of links, ask for the specific spot that would be most appropriate. Next, provide the site owner with the URL you want her to link to—don't leave that to chance. You can also provide HTML code so she can just paste your link into the appropriate place. Make it easy. A logical question: Why should the owner of an established site give an entry-level person like you a coveted link? After all, nobody wants to clutter his site with hundreds of links.

Awards

As I said earlier, a reciprocal link is a type of endorsement, and the longer someone operates a site, and the more popular that site becomes, the more careful he is about the links he offers. One way to get around that is to give someone an award. Everyone likes winning something.

You can create your own awards in your niche. It could be something like "Top 10 Horse-Training Sites". Create a graphic that looks like a trophy or medal, and then contact the websites to tell them they've won or been nominated for this award. Many will happily place the award on their site, with a reciprocal link back to your site.

Obviously, you can't do this if the sites you're targeting are too big to care what you think of them. A mega-site like espn.com isn't going to play ball with someone who made up an award to get a reciprocal link. Which brings me back to the importance of patience. Unless you're already well known in your field, it's going to take time to build credibility, move up in search-engine rankings, and draw high-quality links to your site.

That doesn't mean you should sit back and hope the audience finds you. That's no way to run a business. You can, however, outsource the search for appropriate links you can get now. Search for a qualified freelancer at http://www.elance.com, http://www.guru.com and http://www.brickworkindia.com.

Beware of Link-Farm Scams

Lots of unscrupulous companies troll the Internet looking for easy prey. And if you have new sites, you're seen as fresh meat. One common scam is offering you thousands of links overnight. These scams are commonly known as link farms. Wikipedia defines a link farm as, "Any group of web pages that all hyperlink to every other page in the group. Although some link farms can be created by hand, most are created through automated programs and services. A link farm is a form of spamming the index of a search engine." If you sign up with a link farm, you'll probably get blacklisted from search engines. So stay away. If it sounds too simple and easy, it is.

 **Today's assignment:**

Write your five last pages of your product! Once you're done with that, start building your plan for submitting your squeeze page to directories and building backlinks. Choose three to four key phrases that you most want to focus on for your backlinks.

Using those keyword phrases, submit your squeeze page to at least five different directories. Look for general directories and directories that are related to your market. After you submit your articles, move on to creating a supplemental site that will add backlinks to your main website. Finally, create a links page on your main website and search for at least 10 related websites that you can trade reciprocal links with.

Day 22:
And Beyond...

Let me be the first to offer you congratulations for completing the 21-day plan. Believe it or not, you're way ahead of just about anybody else who wants to do the things you've already begun doing. Very few people take any action to change their course in life and reach their goals. Even fewer go as far as buying a book that promises to tell them how to do it. And only a fraction of those will follow through and complete all the steps in the program.

In fact, if I had to guess right now, I'd say that only a minority of those who buy this product will actually finish it. You're now part of a very small group—a group that includes me and most of the truly successful entrepreneurs in the world today. The first 21 days are just that—the first steps, the beginning of your career in information marketing. Now I'm going to tell you what to do on Day 22 and beyond.

Social Networking

Social networking is revolutionizing the way people meet and communicate online. In the last three years, the use of social networks has jumped through the roof and the result has been a great opportunity for you to connect with your market, build more backlinks and building brand.

There's a new dynamic online, often referred to as Web 2.0. Content that is being produced and shared by communities of volunteers. Wikipedia, for example, allows anyone who registers to create or edit entries. The rest of the community modifies the entries, including edits of the edits, until the content reaches the community's standards for accuracy, clarity, neutrality, and so on. People, who try to use the online encyclopedia for personal promotion, quickly realize that it's hard to get away with it—the community is quick to find and either edit or eliminate that kind of information. Social networking sites are another phenomenon that stress community above all else.

You can—and should—use social networks to promote yourself and market your products. The most popular right now are:

http://www.facebook.com
http://www.twitter.com
http://www.linkedin.com

You may also be able to find wikis and other social networking platforms that are directly connected with your topic and your market. Start with these three at least, and then expand as you see fit. Social networking sites will allow you to interact with users and post dynamic types of content.

Social bookmarking sites are also very helpful in your promotional efforts. The following social bookmarking sites should be at the top of your list:

http://www.digg.com
http://www.reddit.comn
http://www.stumbleupon.com
http://www.furl.com
http://del.icio.us

A final type of social networking site, I'll call a Web 2.0 sites. These sites allow you create a small webpage with a unique URL and add text, pictures and links. The Web 2.0 sites are free to use and are simple to set up. You can create one for each of your main keywords in a matter of just a few hours. Register and create pages on the following sites:

http://www.squidoo.com
http://www.hubpages.com
http://www.blogspot.com
http://www.scribd.com
http://www.gather.com

While each site has its own features and customs, there are some basic steps you can take to join in:

- **Create a free account:** Most sites allow you to register for free, so set up an account. Take advantage of the free exposure and search-engine placement these accounts can get you.

- **Don't be bashful:** If the site allows you to create a full profile, do it. Add photos if you can, as well as descriptions of your products, if that's allowed.

- **Post your links:** Social networking sites like facebook.com allow you to add links back to your own sites. You can also use bookmarking sites (like digg.com) to link back to articles and blog posts on your own sites.

- **Post comments:** I discussed this earlier in the book, but it applies here as well. Leave comments wherever you can, with your signature line offering a link back to your main website. Just make sure your comments are relevant, and won't be construed as spam.

What the Future Holds ...

It's really an exciting time to market yourself online. As soon as you feel you've gotten ahead of the curve, you realize you've fallen behind an entirely different curve. There's always something new to learn about marketing your business. One of my favorite sites for keeping up with the changes is http://www.go2web20.net, a directory of all these cutting-edge sites. Mashable (http://www.mashable.com) is also a good site to use to stay on top of new social networking sites and tips.

How to Get Rich, and Stay Rich

Not everyone who creates and markets information products online will get rich. It's mathematically impossible for it to work out that way. Some will, of course. I hope you're one of them, if that's your goal. Some will be happy to create a nice side income, and that's great. Some will be disappointed. I'd like to say that everyone who follows my program will belong to the first category, but it can't possibly work out that way. Your ultimate success depends on your talent, the size and spending habits of the market you've decided to target, and the amount of competition within that market.

Bonus Tips

The entire point of the coaching program was to get you to create and market a single product. If you stop there, you'll get whatever that single product brings you. Chances are it won't bring you wealth. Real success comes when you develop a passion for creating and marketing information products, do it full-time and with all your creative energy, and build your business year after year. If that happens, the amount of money you can make is unlimited.

Just look at me - A few years ago, I was a gym teacher in the Bronx. Now I have complete financial independence! I didn't take any special classes that taught me how to do this, I don't have any unique computer skills, and you already know that my master's degree is in exercise science, not business administration.

I worked hard, of course, but that was easy, since I love what I do. If I had to pick one thing that sets me apart, it's the fact that I created valuable products and programs for my customers and clients. Since no single product or program can solve every problem or meet every need, the key to your success is to create products in different forms, with different price points, to solve the problems of customers with different needs and different resources they're willing to spend to address those needs.

That's why your most promising strategy is to create your own information empire. It will probably include many of these types of products:

- **Books on CD (or audio download):** You can read your own book and record it to a CD, or offer it as a downloadable MP3.
- **Interview on CD (or audio download):** Record interviews with other experts in your market niche, and offer them as a CD, or a multiple-CD set.
- **Interviews (text):** Have the interviews transcribed into a book, e-book, or manual.
- **Case studies on CD (or audio download):** Interview other people who have achieved success in your target market.
- **Case studies (text):** Have the case studies transcribed and put them into a book, e-book, or manual.
- **Workshop or seminar on DVD:** Do a live lecture or demonstration, and record the full program on DVD.

- **Workshop or seminar on audio CD:** Do a live lecture or demonstration, and record the full program on audio CD.

- **Workshop or seminar (big kit):** Combine the audio CDs and DVDs of your live event, and now you have an expensive kit to sell. As a bonus, you can also have all the audio transcribed and include that text as a follow-along manual.

- **Book from the public domain:** Find publications that have expired copyrights. You can reprint them and keep 100 percent of the profits.

- **Private-label products:** You can purchase the rights to resell information products, and put them under your own label or brand.

- **Resell or reprint rights:** Purchase resell or reprint rights of products to sell to your customers—easy profit with very little work on your part.

- **Build a membership site:** This is my favorite information product. Charge yearly or monthly fees to allow access to your best content online. (For an example, check out one of mine: membersitebootcamp.com.)

- **Coaching program:** Offer monthly coaching programs, which give clients private phone conversations with you, group teleseminars, or some combination.

- **"Best of" product:** Combine all of your best articles and/or interviews into a Best of ... book or kit.

- **Teleseminars on CD (or audio download):** Promote a live teleseminar, and sell the recordings on audio CD or as an audio download.

- **Screenshot videos:** Use a program such as Camtasia (techsmith.com) to record your computer screen. This is great for software tutorials.

- **Live boot camps:** Run a multiday event in your market niche. Bring in guest speakers, and take a percentage of all the back-of-the-room product sales. I know some marketers who make seven figures with a single weekend-long boot camp.

- **Resource directory:** Compile a list of resources in your target market—vendors, wholesalers, websites, etc. You can sell it as a CD, downloadable file, or printed book.

- **Software:** Hire a programmer to build a software program to your specifications, with unique benefits to your customers and clients. Or you can do like Bill Gates, and buy an existing software program. In his case, it was an operating system called 86-DOS, which he then licensed to IBM, making it the default operating system for personal computers before most people had even heard of PCs. Talk about getting in on the ground floor!

These ideas are just a sample of what you can do with information products. That's what I love about this business—you can always come up with new products, or new ways to package existing products. You might even create an entire new category of products, and I'll have to hire you as my personal coach.

Keep up-to-date with all of the latest updates in the exciting world of "Passion to Profits" at www.ryanlee.com. The site is updated daily with videos, advice and articles that will keep you on the path to freedom. And make sure to signup for my free newsletter and special report called "7 Ways to Double Your Income" at the site.

If you want me to personally help you build your online business, try our Inner Circle Coaching Club.

Try it for JUST $1 at www.ryanlee.com

I wish you much success on your Internet journey…